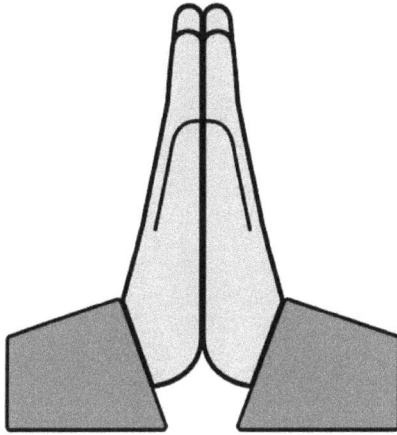

Gratitude

TRUE STORIES OF GRIT, GROWTH, AND GRACE

Edited by Edward McCann

650

READ650 • 1 WRITER. 5 MINUTES. 650 WORDS.

Founder / Editor • Edward McCann
Executive Producer • Richard Kollath
Senior Editor / Literary Ombudsman • Steven Lewis
Editor • Karen Dukess
Editor • David Masello
Editor • Lisa Donati Mayer
Marketing/Communications • Jane Kaupp
Design Director • Diane Fokas
Technical Advisor • Conrad Trautmann
Technical Advisor • Stephen Kaupp
Director of Photography • Kevin O'Connor
Chief Audio Engineer • Jesse Chason
Copy Editor • Shelley Sadler Kenney
Intern • Kerry Lubman

Advisory Committee
Sara Caldwell, Jeremiah Horrigan, Arif Ilahi Khan,
David Masello, Irene O'Garden, John Pielmeier,
Susan Ragusa, James Russek, Angela Derecas Taylor

READ650 | Gratitude

"Piglet noticed that even though he had a very small heart, it could hold a rather large amount of gratitude."

—*A.A. Milne*

I hit a rough patch in my life a couple of years ago and, edging toward despair, I phoned my niece, Jane, to vent and to seek some fresh perspective. Jane—honest, kind, and wise beyond her years—listened patiently while I unloaded my frustrations and grief, then assigned me a task that changed my outlook and my life. "You should start every day," she said, "by writing down five things you're grateful for."

Beginning a gratitude journal was an exercise that altered my thinking—and shifted my focus from what I wish for to what I have. Logging those first five things was easy—my husband Richard, a hot shower, birdsong, blue sky, fresh coffee—but I quickly realized thinking about gratitude makes it grow, naturally displacing darkness and negativity. Gratitude really is the key to a happy life, and the personal stories in this volume demonstrate gratitude in many forms. I'm grateful for this opportunity to present them to you!

Read650 is a literary nonprofit promoting writers through live and digital performances that celebrate the spoken word—a forum organized around single, broad topics featuring two-page, 650-word personal stories that can be performed in five minutes. The recorded performances from our events are added to a growing archive of writers reading their work aloud, with additional planned exposure through podcasts, broadcasts, our YouTube channel, and in printed volumes like the one you hold in your hand.

We feature graduate students and grandparents, and first-timers often share the stage with bestselling authors. It's all about the writing—word choices, the shape of sentences and paragraphs, the arc of a narrative, and the poetry of a unique literary voice. To submit your work or attend our shows, visit our website or Facebook page, and join our mailing list. Tell your friends about us, and please help spread the word about the spoken word.

Ed McCann

Edward McCann, Founder / Editor

READ650.ORG
FACEBOOK.COM/READ650

CONTENTS

Brightness • Judy Andrews / 1

Gratis • Jamie Bernstein / 5

Blessing Them • Ann Casapini / 9

Nicholas and Baby Girl • Minnette Coleman / 13

Tiv • Honor Finnegan / 17

The Gift • Mihai Grunfeld / 21

A Rhyme Scheme • Bert Hornback / 25

Fellow Travelers • Sally Hoskins / 29

To the Chicken • Chebrya Jeffrey / 33

Lucky Penny • Rebecca Kalin / 37

Learning to Love my Ferrari • Janice Kaplan / 41

Apollo's Creed • Matthew Kelly / 45

Fear of Fear of Flying • Beth Levine / 49

The Breathless Day(s) After June 2, 1977 • Steven Lewis / 53

CONTENTS

The Luckiest Bastard • E. Marmer / 57

Wearing My Insides Out • Jane Marx / 61

Ode to Joy • Edward McCann / 65

Every Breath You Take • Malachy McCourt / 69

A Tribute to my Sisters • Ed Meek / 73

Soup • Margarita Meyendorff / 77

Lucy and Old Fred • Anthony Murphy / 81

Two Words • John Pielmeier / 85

The First Day Back • Andi Rosenthal / 89

The Band Room • Leanne Sowul / 93

My First Job • Yvonne Stafford / 97

Turkey • Xavier Trevino / 101

I'm Not Ellen DeGeneres • Frances Tunno / 105

For Things Denied • Sarah Bracey White / 109

Acknowledgments / 113

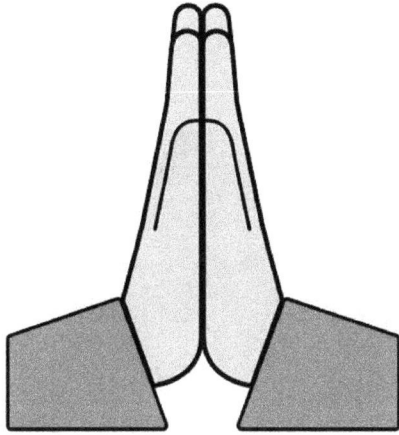

Gratitude

TRUE STORIES OF GRIT, GROWTH, AND GRACE

JUDY C. ANDREWS

Judy C. Andrews received a master of arts degree in English/ Creative Writing, and a bachelor of liberal arts and sciences degree from The City College of New York. She has worked as an educator, freelance writer, and editor. As a foster child, she was appointed as a children's advocate by former President Jimmy Carter. Ms. Andrews enjoys writing stories from a thrilling Gullah/Geechee perspective. She is a member of the Harlem Writers Guild. The characters in her novels, *An Ocean of Jewels*, and *A Gift to Treasure*, are foster children, educators, and amateur sleuths who seek ways to rectify dangerous situations or experiences in the predominantly African American communities of her fictional towns of Creeksville, Georgia, Eva Creek Island, Georgia, and Jewel Park, New York. Her website is BlessedBrown.com.

BRIGHTNESS

Judy C. Andrews

As a child, I experienced the world through thick, bifocal glasses. My fourth-grade English teacher, Mr. Greene, haunted me often. For one semester, he thought I could not read, and I was too embarrassed to tell him that I could not see the board.

I had similar experiences in high school and college, and though I wore contacts when I became a teacher, by the end of each day my eyes were so red that my adorable students playfully, but regularly asked, "Ms. Andrews, what you been smokin'?"

One day I squinted again at sentence number ten that I had written for my students on the Smartboard: "Tariq's sanguine temperament and smile pleased Ms. Andrews."

"Yo, Miss! Why you got *my name* up there?"

Laughter from the class.

Tariq was the last person who I wanted to know my secret. Throughout my teaching career, I had managed to cleverly hide that I was legally blind. Tariq was smart, witty,

1

and could pack a punchline that made people convulse with laughter through a stream of tears, and he seemed to have tremendous confidence about his gifts. Everyone noticed.

I told him, "I thought you would really appreciate seeing your name up in lights, Tariq!" Sunlight kissed the Smart Board with an extra dose of brightness.

"Ain't no light! That's just bright red, outlined by the sun. Sanguine!" The class waited for a comeback.

I said, "I see you've been studying for our vocabulary test this Friday. Tariq, you might want to review the definitions as well as be able to locate the object of that sentence!"

"Oh, you real funny, Miss Andrews. You the object!"

"I am a riot! Yes, you are correct!"

"I know! Plus, you can't see the board. You're right in front of it!"

I inhaled. Tariq was just getting started! He was on to me. His obnoxious cachinnation was a sign for the rest of the students to join him. They did.

More laughter. Loud!

Finally, I whispered, "Ten-minute quiz!"

Complete silence.

Sunlight framed Tariq's face, a shadow to me. He sat near the side of the Smart Board.

Tariq stammered, "N-No, Miss. That ain't fair!"

Smiling, I said, "Okay, Tariq. Let's see what happens after I grade your test on Friday!" His fourteen-year old wisdom never surprised me.

He yelled, "Imma' bust it out, Miss!"

"I am certain you will!"

"That's right, Miss."

"Okay. No quiz, but test, this Friday!"

Sighs of relief echoed.

I spent the weekend marking exams. I tried to contain my excitement as I awaited my appointment for cataract surgery on my left eye that following Monday. Surgery was completed on my right eye the next day, Tuesday.

My world was now filled with an exquisite, miraculous gift: the joy of heavenly sight! The taxi ride on the Manhattan Bridge from my doctor's office to my Brooklyn home was mesmerizing as I observed New York City's spacious skyline and the picturesque East River. I couldn't wait to see my students! I cried. Wednesday, I rested.

I no longer had to fantasize about clearly reading subtitles, menus, or even Smartboards from the back of my classroom. I was able to recognize, from a distance, people I loved.

On Thursday of that thrilling week, I briefly took a seat at my desk in the front of the room. I chuckled as I scanned the face of each child. The joy of every countenance delighted me, from the blue eye-shadow Marissa wore, to LaQuan's braces when he spoke. Jennifer had dimples! I noticed how Jabari's gray eyes sparkled at a correct answer. I peeked at Tariq, and I gleefully read small letters on his T-shirt, "Superstar." He sat with his group members in the back of the room to work on sentence structure in preparation for his next exam. He had gotten 100 on his test. He smiled, clairvoyantly, as he showed it to his friend.

JAMIE BERNSTEIN

Jamie Bernstein is an author, broadcaster, filmmaker, and concert narrator. In addition to writing her many articles and concert narrations, Jamie travels extensively, speaking about music as well as about her father, composer and conductor Leonard Bernstein. Jamie's film documentary, "Crescendo! The Power of Music" has won numerous prizes, and is now viewable on iTunes. Jamie's memoir, *Famous Father Girl*, was published by HarperCollins in June of 2018, and was released in paperback in June 2019. You can learn more about Jamie's multifaceted life on her website: jamiebernstein.net.

GRATIS

Jamie Bernstein

By now, in my mid-sixties, I've journeyed along the familiar human landscape of ups and downs: marriage, death of parents, childbirth (twice), breast cancer (twice), divorce, professional failures and successes, all the many mile-markers. There are advantages to reaching this age: for example, to have ceased being an erotic object to men. No more lascivious glances, wolf whistles, or subway feel-ups. There is power in knowing you can make yourself invisible in public: just some generic, diminutive, middle aged woman, darting along in her dark colors. Smoke-gray ninja.

Occasionally I've mused that another romantic relationship might possibly still be out there waiting for me. I have curiosity, and energy; I can pull myself together, look good enough—even if it does take, as my friends are tired of hearing me say, twice the effort for half the results.

But in the next breath I'd wonder: how would I feel about putting this irreversibly disintegrating body back in action? And would I even remember how stuff worked?

Maybe I'm better off with the morning snuggles of my dog—who, in almost all respects, is the best bed companion I've ever had.

On holidays my extended family—and all our dogs—nestle together in the old place in Connecticut. Thanksgiving is our favorite: no religion, no presents, just close kin, lots of food, and all the heartfelt thank-yous.

Next best is Passover—the Jewish Thanksgiving—featuring more family, feasting, and thanks (albeit tinged with those problematic assertions about being "the chosen people"). Everyone's favorite Seder song is "Dayenu" – translated as "it would have been enough." An excerpt:

If He had split the sea for us, and had not taken us through it on dry land — Dayenu!

If He had taken us through the sea on dry land, and had not drowned our oppressors in it — Dayenu!

And so on, for many verses, none of which we could ever properly reproduce in Hebrew – but oh, how heartily we chimed in on the catchy "Da, da, ye-nu, Da, da, ye-nu!" chorus.

My life has been very full lately: at least a hundred Dayenu verses of more-than-enough. So I don't ask for additional goodies; I lean toward thank you, not please, in my prayers. (Anyway, I don't subscribe to begging a deity for favors.)

Then the unexpected, unprayed-for thing happened. A person came back into my life, a person from forty-one years ago. Once this thunderbolt of reconnection was upon me, it seemed inevitable, essential. And I *did* remember how stuff worked. My body (my rickety old body!) had found its completing piece—like the two rocks I once found on the beach that seamlessly conjoined when I slid their irregular surfaces against each other in just a certain way.

There's a pure, present-tense rigor to gratitude. It requires discipline; it's a practice. The trick for me, now, is to embrace this new embarrassment of riches, to repel the toxic shadow of "do I deserve this?" (That shadow can shut a heart right down.) I'll try to keep out of my own way: accept what fell to earth and landed in my lap, unasked-for. Unpaid-for. *Gratis.*

When we're suffused in the goodness of life, we have the overwhelming urge to thank *somebody*. Yet I don't really believe that some discrete entity is arranging my circumstances. I sense it more as the universe wheeling around—for no reason, or reasons far beyond my understanding—and depositing me, for a while at least, in the light-drenched place where I am now.

ANN CASAPINI

Ann Casapini, a yoga and meditation instructor since 1995, also loves to write, sing and dance salsa. She has been published in *Still Point Arts Quarterly;* Dunes Review; *The Sun;* Awakened Voices Blog: The Nightingale; *Medusa's Laugh Press: Microtext Anthology 3;* Intima: A Journal of Narrative Medicine; Scablands Books: Weird Sisters; *and The Afterlife of Discarded Objects,* a collective storytelling project. Ann is a repeat contributor to both Read650 and Military Experience & the Arts' on-line journal: As You Were. Ann was a finalist in the *Southampton Review*'s 2017 TSR Short, Short Fiction contest and received an Honorable Mention in *The Westchester Review's* 2016 Flash Fiction contest. She studies writing with Steven Lewis and lives in Tuckahoe, New York.

BLESSING THEM

Ann Casapini

After my brother got arrested, first came denial. *You wouldn't do this.* Then deep sadness. *What about your sweet dog? What about Christmas?* Then shame. *What will we tell our relatives, friends, neighbors?* Finally, a numbness and loss of interest in my own life. I missed two weeks of work. I lost weight. I was having trouble concentrating.

When I first started going to the prison to visit him, I raged against the guards. I hated their sullen faces, despised them when they smiled or made small talk. I freaked out when they made me wait as they looked up my brother's ID number, or made me wait to get my locker key, then made me wait again to walk through the metal detectors. I reacted to every delay with a tightening in my chest and throat. By the time they were finally ready to escort me in, my saliva had turned bitter.

And after all that, sometimes the visiting room would be empty. The guards would tell me they had "forgotten" to call my brother down to see me, which meant I had to endure another wasted half hour of precious contact time, waiting for them to get him.

By then, my adrenaline levels would be so pumped up, I'd have hot flashes, a racing heart, trembling hands. I'd have to stifle a panicky desire to bolt out of the place.

I was falling apart. I needed help. So, I started to see a counselor.

She told me I should try and "Bless the guards." My response? *No effen way! She's crazy.* But I was desperate. My anger, sadness and helplessness were eating me up.

So, the night before my next visit, I sat on a cushion and tried it. A memory of a particularly irritating guard came into my mind. He was so insensitive to the families of prisoners that he actually wore a gold tie clip in the design of tiny handcuffs. I wanted to scream. *Bless this guy?* It made my body quake. *No, I can't do this.* Instead, I sobbed.

The next day, once inside the prison, I forced myself to silently bless each male or female guard I saw. *Bless you for signing me in.* I gagged. *Bless you for giving me the key to the ladies room.* I felt nauseous but I silently kept repeating "Bless you." "Bless you." "Bless you."

After a few anguished attempts, it felt like a crowbar had been used to pry open the hard casing around my heart, revealing the tender inside. Having blamed the guards for accepting what I viewed as offensive jobs, I began to see how they were just small cogs in the wheels of our country's vast incarceration system. I realized I could have empathy for the staff who were "free" but who did not necessarily have a choice of other employment in their hometowns, the staff who spent forty to sixty hours of their valuable lives every week, for years, inside the prison walls. Their working day was surrounded by tremendous sadness and violence.

After that day, whenever I visited my brother, I blessed everyone I encountered. And that practice, perhaps the hardest thing I'd ever done, gave me a gift of compassion. Even though I didn't want it. Even though I didn't know I desperately needed it.

I began to allow myself to feel joy, to not feel guilty that I was out in the world while my brother was not, to stop hiding the shame I carried as the sister to a brother who was serving decades in a federal facility. I began to sleep better at night. I felt compassion for myself and all human beings who suffer.

And when I would exit the prison's drab high walls and barbed wire fences, I'd see blue sky, breathe in the smell of fresh cut grass and allow myself to fully exhale with gratitude.

11

MINNETTE COLEMAN

Minnette Coleman, a member of the prestigious Harlem Writers Guild, was born and raised in Atlanta, Georgia, and stared writing short stories and poems at an early age. She wrote for *Atlanta Teen Magazine*, and she wrote entertainment reviews for the *Atlanta Daily World*. While majoring in Drama and Speech at Guilford College in Greensboro, North Carolina, she was a frequent contributor to the college newspaper, the award-winning *Guilfordian*. She is the author or three historical novels, *The Blacksmith's Daughter, No Death by Unknown Hands*, and *The Tree: A Journey to Freedom*. A resident of Harlem, she has been published in the *Quaker Higher Education Journal* as well as the *Killens Review of Arts and Letters*.

NICHOLAS AND BABY GIRL

Minnette Coleman

My nephew is looking for a bow to decorate a gift and he knows one is trapped in the clutter of my mother's craft paraphernalia. As he complains, pilfering through battered shopping bags and bruised corrugated boxes stuffed under the table that is her creative headquarters, I listen, afraid to interrupt this odd couple's domestic drama.

"If you were organized, grandmamma, I could find it."

She eyes his rummaging from her recliner. "Nicholas, you know I need some bins. I'll get some with my birthday money."

He pulls out the remains of a misshapen plastic box, probably melted by mama's glue gun, pleading, "Can I toss this?"

"No, I might need it."

For what, I wonder? But he doesn't argue. Instead, he says, "I just need a bow, Baby Girl. I'll give it back."

Three things come to mind. How's he gonna give a gift then give my mother, the Queen of Crafts, back her bow?

Why didn't she say she needed storage containers for her birthday, the reason I'm in town? And when did he start calling his ninety-four-year-old grandmother Baby Girl?

After my dad died, my thirty-something nephew moved in so Mama wouldn't be alone. This soon became the best relationship he had with any woman, save his mother. Nicholas tells spouse-seekers he must take care of his grandmother. They are immediately enraptured, proclaiming this would-be Lothario a piece of Jesus, as the Southern saying goes. Mama says he isn't. Whenever I visit, I can't be sure who is most appreciative of this relationship: Mama, who reminds me on nightly calls what a joy and pain Nicholas can be, or me, usually worried about her some eight hundred miles away, or my nephew, who has a built-in excuse for his bachelorhood. Whatever the case it's obvious Nicholas and Baby Girl have things worked out.

When I first arrived, he appeared with a basket of clean laundry. Mama frowned: "Boy, I don't want to fold up clothes."

He pulled out bright red boxer shorts. "Baby girl, does this look like your underwear? No, it's mine. Your clothes are still washing."

"Well, thank you," she huffed then smiled.

When she was able, she'd cook for him while he cleaned the basement or raked the back yard. Nowadays senior meals are delivered. Still he treats Mama to fried fish lunches, Wendy's Frostys, and bags of pork rinds. He takes her to the bank, to Scrabble club and does the grocery shopping, making sure she has Coca Cola, her favorite beverage. Once he brought home a large bottle of generic cola. "Did I ask for this mess? It's nothing but flavorless, brown water. Take it right back and get me a six pack of the 'real thing.'" That was one mistake he never made again.

Finally, Nicholas finds a bow, says "Thanks, Baby Girl," and disappears down the hall.

I know what happens next will be more entertaining than the hours of Court TV we've been watching, their guilty pleasure on his days off. Like beauty contest commentators they discuss the bad wigs, wardrobe choices, and dental hygiene of those facing the bench.

"What made her wear that to court?"

"Nothing wrong with wearing a mini-dress."

"Well, I can see her girdle."

"Grandmamma, those are shorts."

"Looks like underwear to me."

Moments later there is a rustle in the hall as Nicholas pushes in a large, plastic, storage bin, blue bow on top. Mama's face brightens like sunshine. He kisses her forehead. "Happy birthday, grandmamma."

When he removes the lid, revealing more containers, her well-manicured hands pat his cheeks.

The canned Cokes, the laundry, the bins. My nephew knows what my mother needs.

In this little piece of heaven, grace overflows even as Mama takes back her bow. "Thank you, Nicholas. Now put this back where you found it."

I smile. He laughs. "Yes ma'am, Baby Girl."

HONOR FINNEGAN

Honor Finnegan has been singing and performing since she was in the first national tour of *Annie*, at the age of 11. As a young adult, she performed with the Improv Olympic, Chicago's premiere venue for improvisational comedy. More recently, Honor won accolades for songwriting and performing folk music. After a dramatic experience in 2016, involving a flash flood in Texas, Honor began writing (mostly) first person essays, and participating in slams at The Moth. She's a preschool educator / special educator, a Heartfulness Meditation trainer, and mother to one adult son. After twenty years in the Big Apple, Honor relocated to Big Nature on the Oregon Coast where she lives in a refurbished 100-year-old train depot on a magical lake in the woods.

TIV

Honor Finnegan

I didn't know a lot about Tiv, but I saw him, as they say, and he saw me. Being seen can save your life, and you never know who's going to see you. Love appears in unexpected places.

I was twelve years old, and in the first national tour of *Annie*. I'd escaped my dysfunctional family in Chicago, mainly my mother, and joined another dysfunctional family, i.e.; the cast on the road. I was in heaven. It was the good life, and I knew it.

I was the swing, which is an understudy for multiple roles. I got to perform a lot, but there was plenty of time for hanging out backstage. Backstage was where the party was. Intrigue, drama, colorful personalities, spontaneous play. The show was fun, but monotonous, scripted. Backstage, I made the rounds like Eloise at the Plaza Hotel. I heard and saw things I probably shouldn't have, but I loved being the observer, and I loved my adult friends. My most beloved were gay men: Wayne, Steve, Moose, Charles and Tiv.

Of course, most of the men in the show were gay. It was theatre, after all, but not all of them were my friends, because gay people, as you may, or may not know, are just people. Some you click with, and some you don't.

Tiv and Charles did make-up and wigs. Tiv had red hair, and a beard, with a handlebar mustache. Edgy, intense, and at times, intimidating, he got a kick out of me, and I, him. I was skilled at edgy people due to my mother. I could handle Tiv. I knew how to stay out of his way when it was busy, how to make him laugh, and when to go in for a hug.

"Here comes Voodoo Vera!" Tiv would say, as I entered the room. Then Charles would start in. The name of the game was making up names for me, based on the notion that I wanted the other girls to get sick so I could go on. Chicken Pox Polly. Florence Influenza. Voodoo Vera was my favorite. The twinkle in their eyes, as they teased, delighted me. I enjoyed being their target, the inspiration for fictional femme fatales. I'd always fancied myself a good witch. I loved it. I loved them.

Years later, as an adult living in Manhattan, I got a call from a friend of Tiv's. Tiv was in the hospital and dying. The friend was sorting through his things, and found some memorabilia pertaining to me. He thought Tiv would appreciate a visit. Could I come to the hospital?

I remembered going to see my father in the hospital when I was eight. He was in a coma and dying, and I sort of went berserk when he didn't recognize me. Since then, I'd avoided hospitals, when at all possible, but now I'd been asked by Tiv's friend, and Tiv had saved something of me, and Tiv was alone, and Tiv was dying.

So, I went to the hospital, and it was not unlike the scene with my father years before. Tiv did recognize me, but he could hardly talk, and I could barely stop crying. I don't think I was much help. He was in a lot of pain. He didn't need me falling apart, but I did try.

Days later, Tiv died, and his friend sent me the memorabilia he'd saved. It was a Voodoo doll. Something I'd put together as a gift to Tiv, when I left the tour. I'd forgotten all about it. Tiv had kept it for thirty years. It was a small beanie baby like figure of a man with a large pearl-headed pin, and it came with instructions, *The Voo Doo Doll Owners Manuel*. I could see why he kept it. Being seen can save your life, and you never know who's going to see you.

Last year, I was pulled from the clutches of death, by a man I'd never met, in a place I didn't understand. I never asked who he slept with, or who he voted for. I never asked Tiv either.

Love appears in unexpected places, and it's love that saves us. Always.

MIHAI GRÜNFELD

Mihai Grünfeld was born in Cluj, Romania, where he lived until age eighteen. In 1969 he and his older brother traveled to Czechoslovakia and from there escaped to Austria. Thus began a journey that took him to Israel, Italy, Sweden, and Canada in search of a home in the West. Settled in the United States, he obtained his PhD from the University of California at Berkeley; since 1987 he has been a professor of Spanish and Latin American Literature at Vassar College. Published books include a 2008 memoir, *Leaving—Memories of Romania*, and another novel that was adapted into the 2017 play *The Dressmaker's Secret*, which enjoyed a month-long sold out run in New York City. He lives with his family in Poughkeepsie, New York.

THE GIFT

Mihai Grünfeld

Once—only once—did my mother open the locks of her memory to tell me a story about Auschwitz. I was ten, and it happened quite unexpectedly, like a precious gift.

A Sunday morning, after breakfast, I was on my way outside to play when I heard Mama's voice from the bedroom. "Misike, come here."

She is sitting on the carpet, leaning against the wall with a soft pillow behind her back, holding a notebook on her lap.

"Sit down here with me. I want to teach you the Hebrew alphabet."

"Now?"

"Please, come and sit."

Bright sunlight pours in through the windows in front of me, lighting up the white crumpled sheets of my parents' unmade beds. Through the open windows I see the tops of the chestnut trees. Mama puts her arm around my shoulders and gently draws me close to her. I feel her warm arm against my skin and snuggle in. She opens the notebook and draws a few strange letters. These letters don't mean much to me, so I ask:

"Mama, would you tell me something about the concentration camps?"

As if waiting for something, she remains quiet. I don't dare move. The warm sunlight pours in through the open windows. Mama puts the notebook on the carpet and pulls me even closer. The morning air feels still around me. I can barely hear her soft dreamy voice despite the perfect stillness, and I don't dare look at her, afraid that she will stop.

"I was taken to Auschwitz during the summer of 1944 and spent the winter in a wooden barrack without any warm clothes. During the day, I worked in a factory, a long way from the barracks. I was hungry all the time."

A faint smile appears on Mama's face as she continues. "I was so hungry that I risked my life to get a bit of extra food."

Mama's voice perks up a little. "One night I got up and snuck out of the barrack. I walked a few steps toward the fence that surrounded our camp, and then I crawled so the guards in the high posts wouldn't see me. A friend had told me about a spot where, through a hole under the barbed-wire fence, I could get out."

"What if the guards saw you?"

"They would have shot me, but I didn't care. I crept slowly into the field by the camp. It was early winter. I started digging the half-frozen ground with my fingers and eventually found a potato. I wiped it clean on my uniform and bit into it. As the piece warmed in my mouth, I chewed. It tasted really good, and I kept it in my mouth for a long time, before I swallowed."

At this moment Mama turns towards me with a faint smile. "Have you ever tasted a raw potato?"

"No."

She stands up, walks to the pantry and returns with a small potato and a knife. She sits down by me and slowly peels the potato, lost in her thoughts, so solemn I don't dare whisper a word. Then she cuts a thin slice and puts it in her mouth. She also cuts me a small piece. It tastes starchy to me, mostly bland and raw. I look at Mama's face as she eats it, very slowly. I expect her to cry, but she doesn't. She is somewhere else, far away.

"That potato tasted so good," she says, "I promised myself that, if I survived and ever got out, I would eat one raw potato every day."

I look at Mama: "Have you been eating a raw potato every day?"

"No, of course not," she says softly. "I don't want to remember anymore what happened there."

I snuggle up to her warm and soft body, hide my tears under her arm, and we remain quiet, looking out the window.

BERT HORNBACK

Bert Hornback is a retired English professor and writer who now lives in Germany. He grew up in a small town in Southern Kentucky, attended the University of Notre Dame, taught for twenty-eight years at the University of Michigan, ran an art gallery in Amsterdam for three years, then migrated to Saarbrucken, Germany where he has lived for the past ten years. He visits his artist sister in Baltimore somewhat regularly.

A RYHME SCHEME

Bert Hornback

As a child, I was fascinated by language--and the things it could do, or that you could do with it. I had a large vocabulary as a little boy--big enough that in first grade, I always got an extra allotment of anagrams so I could spell "Constantinople" and my other big words. But before I got to spelling, I did spoken rhymes. If somebody said "annoy," I would quickly—and loudly—elaborate: "Boy, coy, joy, toy," Sometimes I would add as rhymes both words I didn't know--like "goy" and "loy"--and words that weren't--like "noy," "voy," and "zoy." Or rhymes I shouldn't have made, like "miss" and "piss" or "hit" and "shit."

My great-uncle John, whom everyone called "retarded," had a special gift for rhyming. He loved rhymes, and on Sundays, in the summertime, John was always in charge of making ice cream. As he churned, he chanted

Julius Caesar | Great big geezer
Bumped his head | On an ice-cream freezer.

Only the one verse, but over and over. Fast, when he started, then more slowly as the ice cream started to set. Then, one slow syllable at a time:

Jul-ius Cae-sar / Great big gee-zer
Bumped his head / On an ice cream free-zer.
Jul-ius Cae-sar / Great big—

—and he would stop. It was ready.

Once John baby-sat for me. When it was time for me to go to bed, I told John, and we went upstairs. I got into my pajamas and climbed in bed.

"Now you have to read to me," I said. I showed him my little pile of books. He shuffled through them, and picked one. Then he sat down on my bed, and read:

The dumpdat / Jumped up
And hits the cat / On the hat
With a brick bat / And knocked him flat.
He turned the page / And that's that.
The story of the dumpdat.

There must have been more to it—more rhymes—but that's all I remember.

Several weeks later, my mother's younger sister was my sitter. When bedtime came, I told Billie that she had to read to me.

"Do you have a favorite book?" she asked.

"Yes! The *Story of the Dumpdat*."

She looked through the pile of books. No *Story of the Dumpdat*. I insisted. Billie couldn't find it. And I would not go to sleep unless she read it to me.

When my parents came home, I was still up. Waiting. Billie explained.

"Jerry," my mother said, "you don't have any *Story of the Dumpdat*,"

"Yes I do!"

"I've never seen it."

"John read it to me."

My mother and Billie looked at each other. John couldn't read.

It was John's influence that started my rhyming. Rhyming was a great protection against boredom when I was small. I did a lot of silent rhyming in school. At church, too. The mass was in Latin, in those days, so I had no idea what the priest was saying. But every now and then I would catch the end of a "Dominus Vobiscum" and I would be off: "dum, gum, hum." Or "Amen"--and I'd think "ben, den, pen."

The first poem I ever wrote rather heavily rhymed, and I dedicate it—with gratitude—to John.

KIDS IS TROUBLE
When I grow up / And get so old
That I'll know what I'm doin' / Without bein' told,

I'll never get married / And raise lots of kids:
Pa told me what trouble / Them little kids is.

They'll set in your lap / And rinkle yer clothes
Get in yer hair-- / I guess Pa knows.

Told me, too, though / Kids is a joy,
'Specially the ones / That is born little boys.

But knowin' myself, now, / I think that's a lie
'Bout raisin' them young 'uns / Bein' easy as pie.

So I'm gonna remember, / All through my days
That kids is trouble-- / And trouble don't pay.

SALLY G. HOSKINS

Sally G. Hoskins is a retired college biology professor from City College of the City University of New York, where she developed the CREATE project, aimed at transforming the teaching and learning of biology through a focus on close reading of research reports rather than textbooks. An avid musician, she founded and conducted SHE, a New York City-based women's vocal ensemble. Her essays have appeared in the *New York Times, Newsweek,* and *Science* magazine as well as in a bunch of scientific journals mainly read by fellow nerve-growth and student-learning-measures obsessives.

FELLOW TRAVELERS

Sally G. Hoskins

I descended the stairs of the downtown subway and encountered a giggling hubbub—a herd of six-year-olds escorted by four teachers. As an intensifying metallic screech signaled the approach of a train, they broke into chains of five, each headed by an adult, all holding hands. I was amazed at the poise of the grown-ups. As a retired college biology professor, I know the value of getting students out of some-times-stultifying classrooms. Learning is easier in a more stimulating environment, like the American Museum of Natural History, where my own classes had occasionally convened for a tour guided by a curator. But we never traveled en masse, so I never had to oversee the commute personally. Even with college-age students, I would have worried that someone would break from the jostling pack and get too close to the platform edge. Supervising young kids, I'd have been a basket case.

I was raised by a very careful father, who was great (or terrible, depending on your perspective) at imagining and preparing for worst-case scenarios. I was surely the only child in my Brownie troop who, during nature walks, rather than gathering autumn leaves, listened acutely for the cracking sound that would signal the impending rapid descent of a killer branch. The October I turned nine, Dad taught me his precursor to the yet-to-be invented Heimlich maneuver, since Halloween candy came in all shapes and sizes, including the spherical throat-cloggers that were banned in our house. As I grew up, I obsessed over *Readers' Digest* "Drama in Real Life" stories, imagining how *I* would hold up if stranded alone in a wrecked car for six days with nothing but one box of Cracker Jack (which I would most certainly *not* choke on). My brother's *Boy's Life* magazine had tales of "Scouts in Action," which taught me to MacGyver a splint out of anything from chopsticks to knitting needles, as well as the best way to carry an unconscious person across a stream, and to never, ever, leave home without duct tape. Just in case.

Watching a crowd of schoolchildren inches from the oncoming train inevitably raised my safety hackles, but everyone boarded without incident. Once we were on our way, the kids twirled merrily around the metal poles, and when a seat opened up, two of them bounced into it, twisting to look out the window at the grimy blur. I had forgotten how much *fun* the subway is. Even the teachers seemed to be enjoying the break from classroom tradition, their smiling faces betraying no tension as they chatted with their designated quintet. I flashed back to my own first-grade experience at the school I had walked to every day. Our cherished field trips to Chicago museums involved, rather than public transit, long bus rides during which we were safely containerized. Decades later I still remember those adventures, as I knew these kids would one day.

As it turned out, we all exited at 42nd Street. Everyone eased into the crush of people headed toward the stairs, the children again holding hands in line. I guessed they were going to the Discovery Center; I doubted that Madame Tussaud's Wax Museum would be a New York City Department of Education sanctioned experience. In step with one of the teachers, I broke through my subway armor to acknowledge the challenge of her profession, as well as her grace in action. Catching her eye, I said "You have the most important job in the world, and the least respected. I wish I were a mega-millionaire so I could triple your salary."

She beamed. "It means a lot that you said that. Thank you." We clicked in that moment, teacher to teacher, New Yorker to New Yorker.

Once on the street, I stopped at a newspaper kiosk and bought a Mega Millions ticket. Just in case.

CHEBRYA JEFFREY

An Ohio native, **Chebrya Jeffrey**'s interest in writing started with poetry in early years, but with time, she became increasingly interested in the essay. Referred to as an at-risk youth, Jeffrey credits a religious experience that put her on a different course and then later changed her life. She is a frequent traveler who writes occasionally.

TO THE CHICKEN

Chebrya Jeffrey

The plate was small, a sandy porcelain with a dark green rim. On it the food was economically arranged. I looked it all over before eating: baked chicken, broccoli florets, and roasted potatoes speckled with rosemary. I ate the first bite of chicken without any of the sauces because I wanted to know what it tasted like on its own. It was tender and moist. I was thinking of how strange it was to be putting another animal's body in my mouth and swallowing it, and that you don't get much closer to another living thing than that.

I wasn't supposed to be thinking though. My aim was to focus. The reason was that my thoughts were racing over a recurring, imaginary scenario in which I lose someone or something important to me (i.e. my family dies) and then realize how wrong my priorities had been all along.

I had recently read an article called "The Four States of Mind." The article was riffing off of a book called *Mind Gym* which I hadn't read, but the basic premise was that there were varied orientations of focus, each impacting, or working with others to create, one's state of mind.

In the article, focus was explained as being either external or internal. Internal focus was comprised of attention to inner dialogue, one's own thoughts and interpretations, while external focus included attention to environmental subjects and events. Since my thoughts were incessant and anxiety-producing, I chose to focus on the ever-changing world around me.

I was staring at a fraction of the body of a chicken, and at myself eating it. I was imagining the broccoli and potatoes being picked by farmers from the ground, and that's when it happened. It was unrehearsed. " And thank you to the chicken," I said aloud, "though I know not where from."

Saying thanks for food is not customary for me. It's not that I'm not grateful (I hope). It just often feels like some extraneous insertion into the normal chain of events. Maybe that feeling is rooted in some disconnection between myself and what I eat and where it comes from.

I understand the spirit in which old native traditions resulted in thanks. These people labored through the whole process of turning living things into food to be consumed themselves. But me, I retrieve my food in cardboard packaging, toss it into metal carts or plastic baskets, place it routinely over laser barcode scanners, and exchange it for dollars and coins. My heart rate doesn't even increase, except for anxiety at all the options.

Some people I know pray before meals to give thanks, but it's hard for me to attribute the whole thing to God. I know what I'm involving myself with when I sit down to eat another animal. I have an idea of what happens to the chickens whose end, predetermined, it is to be food at grocery stores. I've seen the slaughterhouse videos. It's not a suffer-free life they lead.

And that's been my dilemma with gratitude! How do I be thankful for the relative good in my life when it's connected to or in the context of the suffering of something else? I've avoided gratitude journals and lists, suggestions from friends and even Oprah, out of fear that in all this feel good gratitude I would forget what sometimes lies on the other side.

When the thank you made its way from my head to my mouth to the air, it wasn't to the gods or to some provisionary force; it was to the chicken. It was a nod to the situation the chicken and I were both in. It was a lament and an appreciation at the same time. Perhaps that's what gratitude really is.

REBECCA KALIN

A lifelong storyteller, **Rebecca Kalin** has worked as an artist and animator, founded and run a successful non-profit, hitchhiked across South America dressed as a boy, made clothes for animals on *Saturday Night Live*, taught scriptwriting to Africans, and wrote four original screenplays and an opera libretto. Now in what is commonly euphemized as retirement, she is finally getting around to writing and illustrating stories from what has admittedly been an interesting life.

LUCKY PENNY

Rebecca Kalin

I never step over a dropped penny. It is a small token of what a big city freely offers. Pick it up, slip it in your pocket and believe that anything can happen at any time. Open heart. Open mind. Once, on West 10th Street, I found four ten-dollar bills in a pile of leaves. On East 83rd Street, I found a gold heart the size of a dime. On East 9th, I found a love letter, and a few weeks later, a live chicken. The best thing I found was an opera conductor on the streets of Brooklyn.

Only one week before, I awoke in the middle of the night with a start. As clear as daylight, a message exploded in my 3 am brain, "*Fire Princess* is supposed to be an opera!" *Fire Princess*: for years my screenplay braved the rollercoaster of false hopes before settling on a dusty shelf. The story—one of obsession, betrayal, poetry and death—was operatically perfect.

I was headed to a trucking warehouse in Dumbo for a performance of *Tosca* when it happened. I had never been to the advised subway stop and when I got out I had no idea where I was. My few fellow riders were beginning to disappear down empty, dimly lit streets, their backs receding by the moment. "Is anyone going to *Tosca*?" I shouted.

A handsome young man stopped and turned around. He raised one finger and said, "I am." We walked together. He introduced himself as a conductor and asked if I was a singer.

"No," I said. "I am a librettist."

"Wonderful!" he said, clapping his hands. "My best friend is a composer looking for a librettist."

Wonderful indeed! Except that I had never written a libretto.

We arranged to meet the next month at a concert where the conductor would be leading a piece by his friend, the composer. I promised to be there. On the designated night, to my great despair, I was down with the flu. I kicked myself for missing the appointment and, in my initial excitement, never asking for contact information.

Then I saw a notice of a Puccini opera to be conducted by my street-found friend. Certainly, *his* best friend would be there. I bought tickets for myself and my husband who, every time I moaned about missing the meeting with my composer, would shake his head, pat my arm and say, "Dear, you *have* no composer."

On the night of the opera, I searched the lobby, orchestra section, loge and balcony, looking for an appropriately aged young man who might be a "best friend."

There were young men on dates, young men on cell phones, young men wearing blue jeans and a timpani player wearing a tux. I could not find the best friend.

After the final curtain, we walked in a gaggle of oper-agoers to the Lexington Avenue station on 103rd Street. The train was crowded, and we all took the pole alongside an elderly Hispanic man. When he got off at 96th, I found myself face to face with the timpani player. I looked at him and he looked at me. I pointed my finger, "Composer?" He pointed his finger, "Librettist?" We fell into each other's arms while my husband's mouth fell open.

I believe that wonderful things happen when we trust that they can happen. Open heart. Open mind. As my compos-er and I work toward the completion of *Fire Princess* the opera, I'm grateful for finding him, a lucky penny indeed.

JANICE KAPLAN

Journalist, TV producer, and writer **Janice Kaplan** is the author of fifteen popular books including the *New York Times* bestseller *The Gratitude Diaries*, which has been translated around the world. Her new book, *The Genius of Women*, will be published in February by Dutton. Janice was the editor-in-chief of *Parade* magazine and the executive producer of the TV Guide Television Group, where she created and produced more than 30 primetime network television specials. She has written for dozens of major magazines and websites and appears frequently on TV shows including *Today* and *Good Morning America*. A popular keynote speaker at events around the country, she graduated magna cum laude from Yale University and won Yale's Murray Fellowship for her writing.

LEARNING TO LOVE MY FERRARI

Janice Kaplan

My idea to live more gratefully began at a New Year's Eve party on the Upper East Side of Manhattan. I should have been happy in my little black dress, but my Spanx were too tight, my heels were too high, and I wanted to get home. Just before midnight, someone turned on the TV, and I observed the revelers in Times Square with awe. I'd had a perfectly nice year, but nothing that made me want to put on a funny hat and dance in the streets. What could possibly happen in the coming year to change that? Winning the lottery might help. But no—then next year I would just complain that my taxes were too high. Move to a tropical island? I would surely grumble about a sunburn.

I suddenly realized that if you wait for events to make you happy, you will be waiting for a very long time. If you change your attitude and perspective, you can be happier immediately. So why not do that? In that moment, I formulated a plan. I would spend a year living gratefully and maybe write a book about it.

    I'd had only one glass of champagne, so the idea still made sense the next morning—and I decided to launch the year by being more grateful to my husband. I have a very nice husband. But I have also been married a very long time. Whether it's a husband, a house, or a shiny new car, you get used to things and stop noticing them. Psychologists call it habituation. A classic response is to keep upping the ante. When the Porsche you yearned for is no longer exciting, get a Ferrari. But after a few days of driving, the new car becomes the baseline of your experience, and you forget why its fancy lines seemed so special in the first place. And cars are easier to trade in than husbands.

    The French novelist Marcel Proust said that the real voyage of discovery "consists not in seeking new landscapes, but in having new eyes." I wanted to bring those fresh eyes to the man with whom I shared my bed, my jokes, and my joint checking account. Rather than wanting more, different, and better, it was time to start appreciating the husband I had, rather than the imaginary cross between Brad Pitt and Bill Gates who would always remember to remove his muddy boots at the door.

    On the Friday night after New Year's, my husband and I headed to our house in the country and as we pulled into the driveway, I turned to him and said, "Thank you for driving."

    He looked at me and said, "I always drive."

    "I know," I replied, "but it's snowy and dark and I'm grateful that you're such a good driver, so thank you."

As the weekend continued, I thanked him several more times—for being kind, for being helpful, and even for being so handsome. He didn't comment, but when we sat down to dinner on Sunday night, he looked at me and said, "Thank you for cooking."

"I always cook!" I said.

But in just one weekend, the vibe between us had started to change. We were noticing each other. We were appreciating.

You think that by being grateful to someone, it's a gift to the other person. But it's really a gift to yourself. Gratitude makes you feel better. It changes your perspective. The biggest regret most of us have in looking back is thinking of all the time wasted being unhappy or angry. I had planned to be grateful to my husband for the first month of my project—that seemed like more than enough. But it brought such joy to our marriage, that I kept it going for the whole year. When the next New Year's rolled around, I hugged my husband at midnight and started to cry.

"I don't want this year of gratitude to end," I told him.

He looked at me and said, "Well, you could try being nice next year, too."

MATTHEW KELLY

Matthew Cole Kelly is a queer playwright, librettist, and screenwriter whose work has garnered nominations for over twenty honors. Previous developmental credits include Abingdon Theatre Company, Luna Stage, Metropolitan Playhouse, HRC Showcase Theatre, CA's Talk Back Theatre, Loose Change Productions, the Makor/Steinhardt Center, Turn Park Art Space, and Occupy Wall Street. Recently, his play, *The Gods of the Ozarks*, received a production by Dublin's AboutFACE Ireland, garnering praise from Ireland's largest newspaper for "explor[ing] profound questions of life and death with a playful touch." Future projects include the opera *Ami & Tami*, translated into Italian for a production at the Teatro Coccia di Novara. Matthew is currently in residence at The New Jersey Play Lab, New York City's Letter of Marque Theater Company, and Floating Tower in Brooklyn.

APOLLO'S CREED

Mathew Kelly

John the Baptist deserved better eyelashes. The sad, sea-foam green wisps lithographed onto the cover of St. Cecilia's Roman Catholic Church bulletin just weren't cutting it. So I did what any concerned, queer five-year-old would do. I fished through my mom's purse, found her mascara, and gave John the lushest lashes this side of the Passaic River.

Whack. There was an unwritten rule in the catechism of Catholic saints. A line of cosmic cosmetic taste one couldn't cross without incurring the wrath of the heavens. This week, it was John's eyelashes. The week before, Elijah's jawline. I would cross the line and an unseen hand would reach down from the heavens and thwack me across the head. Since I was five and living in urban New Jersey in 1989, that hand belonged to an epically awesome Teenage Mutant Ninja Archangel who would descend from the rafters and pommel with the blunt end of his flaming sword. He was the angel who sat sentry over the mass, ringing the heavenly bells that announced the holiest mystery, when the mystical crackers were transformed into the body of Christ.

I spent Monday through Saturday training my reflexes, Karate-Kid style, hoping to catch a glimpse of my archangel critic. But no matter how hard I trained, whenever I spun around all I saw was the scowling face of the octogenarian neighbor who *always* insisted on sitting behind us. Because apparently watching queer five-year-olds stumble their way through the Apostle's Creed reaffirms your faith when you're 85, your dentures are falling out of your face, and you hate the world.

I leaned into my mom's crocheted sweater and whispered, "Is Apollo coming?" It was a legitimate theological query. You see, all my older brother ever watched was *Rocky IV*. And so, I had become obsessed with Apollo Creed. I knew his story arc like the back of my hand. The Russian boxer delivers the fatal blow. Rocky holds Apollo in his arms. And the two almost-but-not-quite kiss. It was beautiful and tragic and the greatest piece of cinematography my five-year-old self had ever beheld.

Why nobody had thought it appropriate to tell me that the Apostle's Creed and Apollo Creed were different things, I'll never understand. For months, I attempted to overlay the gospel atop the plotline of *Rocky IV*. This week, Rocky was Jesus and Apollo was John the Baptist. John was sentenced to death by the USSR's King Herod and the two held one another, almost-but-not-quite kissing. I was convinced that at the climax of the mass—when heavenly bells announced the transformation of the celestial crackers into the body of

Christ—Carl Weathers would smash through the stained-glass window, Kool-Aid-Man style, resplendent in his American flag boxing shorts.

My dreams were shattered the next week when Philip DeSantos, St. Cecilia's altar boy, ran up during recess, the fear of god in his eyes. "I ring the bells!" he cried, tears streaming down his eyes. "Father Frances makes me duck behind the statue of St. Sebastian and ring the bells!" The magnitude of the fraud was too much for his six-year-old self to handle. He collapsed into my arms and we held each other. He was Apollo Creed. I was Rocky. We almost-but-not-quite kissed.

Mom died earlier this year. I sat sentry by her hospice bed, the same age she had been when she let me steal her mascara to draw luscious eyebrows on John the Baptiste. In her final hours, when the end drew near, I did something I never thought I would do. I called St. Cecilia's Roman Catholic Church. Within minutes, a priest was on his way to perform Last Rites. And as I watched the ritual, I heard Philip DeSantos's Eucharist bells and I saw Carl Weathers burst through the hospice room window. And I was grateful, for in that fleeting, painful moment, everything made perfect sense.

BETH LEVINE

Beth Levine is an award-winning freelance writer whose essays have been published in *Oprah* (where this essay originated), *NextTribe, McSweeney's* and *Salon*. She was also once a finalist in the *New Yorker* caption contest. Her website is BethLevine.net.

FEAR OF FEAR OF FLYING

Beth Levine

Recently, a friend asked me if I'd ever been to Israel. Before I could even open my mouth, she added slyly, "Oh, that's right. You can't get on a plane." I think she was trying to be funny.

There was a time when I would have died a thousand deaths: She knows my dirty secret, she's making fun of me, she thinks I'm pathetic; I am, in fact, pathetic. This time, however, I stopped the tape in my head and played a new one. It said, "Everyone has a screw loose somewhere, and having a thing about planes happens to be mine."

You have no idea how hard I've worked to get here.

I've been a fearful flyer since grade school. Once I grew up, I could white-knuckle a flight, even though the months leading up to it were full of panic attacks, sleepless nights, canceling, and rebooking. (And, once we landed, constant worry about the flight back.) Along with fear came self-loathing: I felt defective. Why could everyone else just *do* this? My last flight

49

was in 1986, a quick and uneventful trip from New York to Boston. I haven't flown since.

Oh, I tried, I tried. Cognitive behavioral therapy, classes, tranquilizers, meditation, workbooks. Everything seemed to make it worse. I once got myself admitted to a Yale University airplane phobia study. My first meeting was scheduled for—wait for it—September 11, 2001. Big surprise, I didn't go to the meeting. I didn't go to any subsequent meetings. I gave up, but the self-flagellation didn't stop: "There is something intrinsically wrong with you," I'd tell myself. Then the humiliation that followed each time I had to make up an excuse for why I couldn't get on a plane. I missed weddings, vacations, business meetings that would have propelled me much further in my career. And each time I wiggled my way out of it, I sobbed for days in frustration and shame.

"Look at all the amazing experiences you could be having!" I berated myself.

So, I decided to go have some. On a whim, I auditioned for a show at a community theater. Much to my surprise, I got the part as the cook in *The Man Who Came to Dinner*, then another as Villager #5 in *Fiddler on the Roof*. That one involved singing and dancing (neither of which I do particularly well). Comedy roles followed, where I shamelessly, in industry-speak, ate the scenery. Made a real meal out of it. Now the director has me on speed dial whenever he needs (and I quote) "a whacked-out nut job."

All my friends asked, "Aren't you terrified?" That stopped me short. I, the Queen of Panic, had zero anxiety about—and took much joy in—doing something most people fear. In other words: There were things I could do that other folks couldn't! Maybe I wasn't going to see the Taj Mahal anytime soon, but how many of my friends could blithely play a 90-year-old obese ex-vaudevillian in front of an audience without an ounce of fear?

Life wasn't passing me by because I couldn't get on a plane—it was passing me by because I was obsessing about what I couldn't do instead of rocking the things I could. "Fly or don't fly," I thought, "but don't waste another minute whining about it."

Not long after, while poking around a gift shop, I found a striated brown agate with a word engraved in it: *Gratitude*. It took my breath away. That one word distilled my shift in attitude. For me to pity myself, not to celebrate the talents, strengths, and opportunities I have—well, that would be ungrateful. The rock now sits on my dresser. I think about its message every day. I am not my fears, and my fears are not me. My world is way bigger than that. Curtain up.

STEVEN LEWIS

Steven Lewis is senior editor and literary ombudsman for Read650. He's also a columnist at *Talking Writing*, a member of the Sarah Lawrence College Writing Institute faculty, and a longtime freelancer whose work has been published in the *New York Times*, the *Washington Post*, *Christian Science Monitor*, the *Los Angeles Times*, and many others. Recent novels include *Take This*, *Loving Violet*, and *A Hard Rain*, all from Codhill Press, and he has an extensive backlist of nonfiction which you can peruse on his website, SteveLewisWriter.com. Steve divides his time between his writing space in New Paltz, New York, and Hatteras Island, North Carolina.

THE BREATHLESS DAY(S)
AFTER JUNE 2, 1977

Steven Lewis

Patti is upstairs in the yellow wallpapered bedroom.
She is nursing hours-old Clover Anne, 7 pounds, 6 ounces.
 The sun is high over the Shawangunk Ridge. The
swooning scent of the overgrown lilac at the corner of the
barn. Cael and Nancy and Addie and I are playing some
clumsy version of tag in the back field when I fall flat on my
back with a gasp, the kids giggling like I'm clowning, dancing
around and jumping on me.
 But the truth is I can't catch my breath, can't laugh with
them, the desperate wheeze of a two-pack-a-day addiction to
Lucky Strikes seizing my lungs. So I close my eyes, waiting for
breath to return, and in that breathless moment at the edge of
life, children's laughter swirling all around, I'm thinking how
our family doc stepped aside when the baby girl crowned the
night before ... how I sidled in between her mother's thighs,
held my palm gently against her tiny skull, received her into

my trembling hands, the sweet muck of birth on my fingers, then on my bare arms, on my lips, the scent of life still seeping through my pores as I lay on my back in the field, children squealing, and when I come up to air, I am breathing but still breathless from that baby's first breath.

A few hours after I toss the pack of Luckys into the garbage can by the barn, Clover is sleeping, wrapped in her mother's arms in the upstairs bedroom. My mother is downstairs with the other kids who are waiting for their dinner.

I am sitting in My Hero Pizzeria on Main Street, New Paltz, fiddling with my wedding ring, turning it around and around, pondering this life, this unplanned life, this unplanned life full of grace, this unplanned undeserved life full of grace, this unplanned undeserved inexplicable life full of grace, this frightening and awesome, unplanned and undeserved, wholly inexplicable life full of grace, four kids in eight years, turning and turning the gold band, then slipping it over the knuckle, baby soft flesh underneath, and as I bring my palm up to my face, the weight of her still cradled in my arms, I inhale the birth scent in that pale and tender circle of skin, the two of us, one wailing, the other holding his breath.

•

Forty years later, Patti and I are upstairs in a different home, a warm yellow house deep in the woods, six empty bedrooms, walls cluttered with photographs of an unplanned and undeserved, wholly inexplicable life full of grace. Three more children have come into our lives. Sixteen grandchildren. The old brick house where Clover was born has been sold and resold two or three times. The placenta I buried the next day on Coffey Lane has long ago alchemized into soil. The birch tree I planted over the placenta was blown over in a storm twenty-seven years later, transformed into firewood and a talisman on a cradle I made for that sweet baby's first baby. And the pizzeria is now a Vietnamese restaurant.

Yet I still feel the weight of the infant I held in my hands that June evening, the scent of her birthing still on the baby soft skin under that wedding band, now a golden amulet that has not come off this finger since that ringing moment forty-two years ago. And these days when I lay down in the grass under Bonticou Crag, a mile or so as the peregrine falcon flies from that yellow wallpapered bedroom, chest rising and falling, lungs clear and pink as a newborn, I close my eyes and hear the ancient wheezing, children squealing all around, Clover's first yowl, grateful for the glorious and frightening reminder of the sweet breathlessness of this unexpected, inexplicable life we live.

E. MARMER

Writing has always been a big part of who **E. Marmer** is, but only for the past few years has she been trying to have her work heard and published. In the past, she found other ways of telling people what she thought: as a lawyer, a mom, and a painter. With more time for herself and an even braver, freer voice in middle age, she is following her impulse, her compulsion really, to write. Examples of E. Marmer's narrative essays about family, life lessons and personal experiences can be found on her blog, FreeToNavelGaze.com. One of her pieces, "Declarations" was selected for the Read650 event, "From A to LGBTQ."

THE LUCKIEST BASTARD

E. Marmer

My father Stanley taught me gratitude the way he taught me everything, which is to say, in the fewest words possible. In contrast, when telling a story, or bringing history alive, boy, could he grandstand. His descriptions were drawn out, delicious, *almost* overdone, but not quite. A consummate natural performer, he never once doubted whether he had the crowd while holding court. And yet, when it came to the personal, he withheld the flamboyance. He withheld the unnecessary. My father conveyed the essential nut of a thing—whether a choice, a betrayal, a triumph, a lesson, a wonder—with a simplicity that never ceased to flabbergast me, humble me and convince me that I was getting truth.

That's not to say that he was always direct. Despite his brevity, he could indulge in metaphor, but, even then, it was delivered straightly, pointedly. Once when I brought up the lavish life my aunt had had before my uncle lost his "six-figure" executive job and became a hardscrabble salesman of cheap merchandise from China, he said, "You know the 'Tortoise and the Hare' right?" I waited for it. "I was the tortoise." He said nothing more. And from that, I comprehended all that he wanted me to. Not just about the comeuppance of the arrogant hare, but about the toil and steadiness, the constancy of the tortoise. About allowing that one brief pat on the back and returning to the task at hand.

On the day my father taught me gratitude, however, he delivered a direct declarative sentence. My mother had thrown him a surprise seventy-fifth birthday party, and the assembled guests were clinking their glasses, saying, "Speech! Speech!" My father stood up, and shook his head slowly with lips pursed for a good long pause, so, at first, I thought we would be treated to Stanley as entertainer, to a poem or funny anecdote or maybe a joke thanking my mother for putting up with him all these years.

"I am the luckiest bastard on earth," he said. And he sat down.

Everyone clapped and a few people chuckled, and I wondered if their clapping and chuckling was in affectionate response to what they presumed was understandable awkwardness at such a moment. They knew my dad could be gruff; they knew he wasn't suave. It seemed they wanted to reassure him: "That's okay. We understand you don't know what to say." But I knew my father, in seven words, had said everything. It was all there: his amazement at fifty-three years of marriage to a modest and loving woman, who built their entire social fabric and cared enough about him to throw this party; his pride and relief that his three grown daughters, who fussed over him, turned out to be accomplished, well-adjusted people he didn't have to worry about; his pleasure at grand-children in varying stages of development, the sixteen-year streak of girls finally, *finally* broken with a boy; satisfaction in the restaurant catering paid for in full with the fruits of his and my mother's labors; even anticipation of his accustomed evening in his recliner with a book and a pipe, and his fat belly.

All of those things were there, and something more, the essential bedrock for gratitude. My father told us that he wasn't entitled to any of it. He was the "luckiest bastard," just a random guy, a *shmo*, a tortoise, a self-educated beat cop for thirty years who got to come home to a hot meal and three girls being raised right by his beautiful, capable wife, she a re-spected teacher to boot. It wasn't luck, of course, but a bounty collected, earned, one small decision, one small commitment at a time. He didn't see it that way, though. His humility and astonishment at what he considered sheer dumb luck formed the best blueprint for gratitude I would ever receive.

I follow it still.

JANE MARX

Jane Marx began her career as a tenth-grade social studies teacher. She then switched to publishing and worked as a social science editor at Random House. Next, she became a student at the American Academy of Dramatic Arts. She's been a self-employed New York City tour guide for close to forty years and a storyteller, stand-up comic, actor, writer and sometime model. She's written and performed two solo plays, *A Coffin Turning Clockwise: A Comedy in Real Time* (2017) and *'Til My Last Breath* (2018) both produced by Artistic New Directions Theatre Company. She's also the subject of Caroline Macfarlane's documentary *Falling Forward* (2019) and the model in a short video showing the new collection of Corey Moranis' jewelry. Her website is JaneMarx.com.

WEARING MY INSIDES OUT

Jane Marx

Orange gives me life. If it were a person, I'd show that hue my gratitude. But as it's part of a larger whole, the color spectrum, I'm thankful for prisms, for they disperse light. We're here on this earth to emit our true colors. How to find my color and express it is my plight. Maybe that's why rainbows taunt me. My gut tells me, "In there is you."

That remains unclear to me until one day, on the street, I'm stopped by a stranger. "Forgive me, I have to ask," she says. "Are you a funeral director? In my eyes you look dreadful."

Transfixed by her frank interest in me, I take no offense. She's reading me like a sign. I'm at odds with myself for reasons unknown. "Shame on you," she continues. "You're committing a crime by burying yourself in navy, black, gray, as if you're wearing a shroud. "

Then comes the *real* shocker. "No part of you looks alive. You're worthy of full exposure. You're golden. Your skin, eyes, teeth are yellow. I can spot an "autumn" far away. I'm a 'Color Me Beautiful' expert. People pay big bucks to hear what I'm giving you for nothing."

I want her to go on. I give her a hug. She pats both shoulders and whispers, "Orange," and disappears.

That word resonates with me. As if in a trance, I go home and throw everything out of my closet, drawers, my hat boxes, even the silver adornments from my jewelry box. Then something happens. The hyperactivity inside my head stops. I concentrate on the seemingly endless shades of orange out there. Fresh orange, burnt orange, blaze orange, carrot orange, peachy orange, yellow orange, tangerine, safety orange, goldenrod, vermillion. My excitement rises. I go shopping, to find things that appeal to me emotionally.

There, hanging on a rack, is an orange curly-lamb jacket. I laugh, try it on, buy it, and go out the door. Greeted on the street with a flurry of shouts, I'm surprised and disconcerted. "Hey there. Big Bird." Those sillies, I think. "I'm in sunrise orange." I've become a purist in the naming of the shades. But what's really new for me is that I'm continually being noticed. A reporter for the David Letterman Show stops me. He puts a microphone to my face wanting to know my thoughts on New Year's resolutions. "I'm against them." I get 31 seconds of airtime on the show that night.

This exposure ignites my creative juices. I buy a bright orange boa. It's portable. It's versatile. It goes with everything.

This new accessory lands my photo on the blog *Advanced Style*—although "Advanced" refers to the wearer being old. But I am 75. I go often now into the Whitney Museum gift shop to check out my image on a poster there grouped with others half my age and younger. On another occasion, a marketing director for a sportswear line admires my outfit, and suddenly I'm garbed in an apricot sweatshirt draped over an orange-peel dress. Then I get busy experimenting, adding red, yellow, green, and watch other people's eyes linger on me. A thirty-something woman stalks me for me three blocks. I'm more than self-conscious. I turn to ask her why she's following me.

"I'm accumulating evidence," she says. "You're proving my point that age is energy. I want you as the model for a video I'm making that shows my collection of Lucite jewelry. This year I'm featuring turquoise and amber."

I tell her I'm wrong for her audience. I'll be a distraction, turning her endeavor into a farce. She's adamant. "I'm all about inclusivity. Everyone, young or old, can wear what I make. Besides, it's not just your attire. You have an incandescent spark the camera will pick up."

Inside my personal prism, I'd call that color orange flame, which is self-lit.

EDWARD McCANN

Edward McCann is an award-winning writer/producer and the founder and editor of *Read650*, celebrating the spoken word with live events in New York City and elsewhere. A regular feature writer for *Milieu* and a long-time contributing editor to *Country Living*, his features and essays have been published in many literary journals, anthologies, and national magazines, including *Better Homes & Gardens*, *Good Housekeeping*, *The Irish Echo*, *The Sun*, and others. His essay, "Pregnant Again," was selected for the anthology, *Listen to Your Mother*, published by Penguin. He lives and writes in a pastoral spot about eighty miles north of New York City and is at work on a collection of essays about life in the Hudson Valley.

ODE TO JOY

Edward McCann

It's a cool, early June morning in Yosemite National Park. When I step out of our cabin, dappled light is spilling across the grass and mulched pathways and I hear songbirds and the distant roar of the falls.

I've visited Yosemite dozens of times in fall and winter, but spring holds many surprises: flowering white dogwoods, blue lupines, orange wallflowers—even a young cinnamon bear, browsing beside the road. The Merced River, fed by melting backcountry snow, looks drinkable, and the falls flow over high granite walls with a volume rarely seen in November.

My partner Richard and I, hotel designers, are here, as usual, for work. But today, attired in orange life jackets, we're rafting on the Merced with our friend Brett, manager of the Ahwahnee Hotel, his eleven-year-old son, Max, and his nine-year-old daughter, Helen, traveling in an inflatable green boat we portage across the road to the river.

Though the day is warm, stepping into the icy, calf-deep water takes my breath away.

Brett and I are the oar men; and, with just a few strokes, we're mid-channel, traveling at a speedy clip. Initially focused on rowing and steering, I quickly realize the current does most of the work, even as it twirls our raft like a floating leaf. Cruising the Merced on a late spring morning with sunlight glinting off the water, I'm awestruck and grinning, seeing the valley the way I imagine the Ahwahneechee once did.

Something resembling white lilac is blooming on the far shore, its blossoms contrasting on a background of deep and bright greens. I inhale an earthy, intoxicating fragrance, like balsam and jasmine, though neither grows here, a scent that changes as we travel, adding notes of wood smoke and sweet, decaying leaves. Each bend in our journey downriver offers new views of rock faces, waterfalls, and meadows; of grazing deer and scampering chipmunks, of jays, robins, and juncos flitting above. Yosemite's iconic, greatest hits are here: postcard-ready views of El Capitan, Half Dome, and Yosemite Falls. To a middle-aged New Yorker like me who first saw these things through a 3-D View Master, it's breathtaking. But to Max, who's lived here since birth, this is simply his backyard. He leaps and dives off the raft dozens of times, bouncing off the sidewall like a diving board and slipping back aboard easily as an otter.

Out on the prow, I dangle my legs in the crystal water, steering around downed trees and boulders, as fascinated by the topography beneath the surface of the river as I am with the landscape above; the trout swimming beneath us seem illuminated and magnified.

At a narrow, sandy beach, we sit on a log sharing pretzels and cold, sweet cherries, tossing stems and pits into a hole in the sand while watching other rafters float by. Before continuing downstream, I walk through a clear, shallow channel to a pebbly sandbar sprouting colonies of grassy sedge; as black and white tiger butterflies flutter around us, Helen makes mud castles and Max hurls driftwood into the swirling currents.

Like Max, I can't resist a dip before we go. Leaving my hat, sunglasses, and life preserver on shore, I walk into the frigid river until I'm waist deep—water so cold that, after a moment, it begins feeling hot. I turn slowly and completely around, drinking in the extraordinary beauty I can see from just this one place while reflecting on the sequence of events that brought Richard and me to the Yosemite Valley for the first time, three thousand miles from our Hudson Valley home. I spot those butterflies again just as I dive beneath the river's surface. The very next second, I explode out of the water and walk against the current back to shore, never feeling more grateful to be alive than I do right now, in this moment, in this blazing sun, in this icy river.

MALACHY McCOURT

Malachy McCourt was born in Brooklyn but raised from age three in Limerick, Ireland. Returning to New York at twenty, he worked manual jobs until becoming an actor, a career including roles on Broadway, off-Broadway, on television, and in film. He's been published in *New York Newsday*, *National Geographic*, the *New York Times* and elsewhere. With brother, Frank, he co-authored the play *A Couple of Blaguards* and has written his own New York Times bestselling memoir, *A Monk Swimming*. Other books include a second memoir, *Singing My Him Song*, *Danny Boy*, *The Claddagh Ring*, *Voices of Ireland*, an anthology, and *Malachy McCourt's History of Ireland*. Happily married to Diana for more than four decades, his most recent book is entitled, *Death Need Not Be Fatal*.

EVERY BREATH YOU TAKE

Malachy McCourt

Two people die every second in our world. That's 120 in every one minute. In the five minutes allotted writers on the Read650 stage, six hundred people will have died.

I am eighty-eight years old and in the departure lounge; when I awake in the morn or indeed anytime and perceive a ceiling in my purview I breathe a thankful sigh and lounge for as long as necessary and then I arise, grateful to be alive.

However, if there is a coffin lid within six inches of my proboscis it will probably occur to me that there is no point in attempting to arise and pretending to be alive.

So what is gratitude all about?

First, I am grateful that my parents did what is sometimes referred to as "It." If my parents didn't do "It," I wouldn't be here this day.

Second, most of us begin life when some stranger gives us a whack on the arse to jump-start our breathing.

A person living to 80 will take 673 million breaths up from the 960 breaths he or she will take in the average hour. I am grateful for that first breath of life.

Third, I am grateful that strange fate placed me in Brooklyn, New York on the date of my birth, 20th of September 1931, instead of the Trans-Atlantic crossing to Ireland where our family was bedeviled by disease, despair and child death. In Ireland we were poverty stricken. Poverty is a disease that motivates people like me to be resourceful, cunning, devious in the survival game of life. Some of us acted like tough guys as did my brother Frank. He was gruff fearless and even though of slight build he intimidated bigger tougher kids who were bullies. I opted for the smiling charmer route as I had that rare physical quality of having all my teeth shiny and white. The women liked my bright smiling face, my respectful attitude; not knowing that behind this charming boyo was me figuring out what I could gain from the encounter pennies, sweets, or cakes. So I am grateful I learned to survive.

Mostly, though, I am filled with gratitude for finding love with my beloved Diana. Gratitude seems such a mild word in the lexicon of our romance. In the maleness of Irish history expressing love could be considered sissy-ish, not to mention weak, except when referring to sports teams or where to get the best pint of Guinness stout. Irishmen never express love for their spouses or for whatever blessings she brings to their lives. Neither do they ever refer to their wives by name, as in *She is always late with my tea. She never does my shirts right. She is always complaining about me having a pint.*

I am eternally grateful to Diana.

I am also grateful for the companionship of my three brothers Frank, Mike, and Alphie and the affection the peace, the love we found in each other before they died. I am blessed with four grown offspring Siobhan, Malachy, Conor and Cormac all who give my heart a warm embrace when I think of them. I adore my stepdaughter Nina who opened up my mind to developmental disabilities with her warrior-like reaction to the horrors of institutional life at Willowbrook.

I delight at being a grandfather to nine human beings, each of whom warms my heart!

And at the end of each day, I am grateful that I live among people who tolerate books and essays by an uneducated, semi-literate lover of family, admirer of mountains, and delighter of living one day, one hour—even one breath—at a time.

ED MEEK

Ed Meek writes poetry, fiction, articles and book reviews. *High Tide* is his fourth book of poems. *Luck,* a collection of his short stories, came out in 2017. He has been published in *The Sun,* the *Paris Review,* the *North American Review,* the *Boston Globe,* and NPR's *Cognoscenti.* He teaches creative writing, helps adults prepare for the high school equivalency exam, and in his spare time, walks his dog, Mookie.

A TRIBUTE TO MY SISTERS

Ed Meek

My two sisters, Susan and Dottie, work with the hospice nurse to give my father a sponge bath. Susan is a nurse. She's taken leave from work to care for my father just as my wife's sister had taken care of her mother, and my friend's sisters took care of their mothers.

My father is skeletal. Ribs protrude like the rungs of a ladder. His legs wooden and shiny as if shellacked. When he breathes, there's a rattle.

Two weeks prior, Susan had an ambulance deliver my father to her apartment from a nursing rehab. The doctors said it was a matter of days before he would pass away. My father had stopped eating. His doctors wanted to put in a feeding tube, but my dad was still mentally sharp and he was adamant about not having one—no feeding tube, and "do not resuscitate." My father, my sisters and I had all learned from our experience with my mother.

My mother had gone into the hospital for an operation on her kidneys but complications ensued. She had her gall bladder removed; then she needed an operation on her heart. One day we walked into the hospital to find her hooked up to a feeding tube despite the fact that we had told her doctor she did not want one. "It could help her recover," he said to us. My sisters convinced my dad to allow it.

My mother did not recover. Instead, over a period of months she slowly died while being shuffled between the hospital and a nursing home. The experts counseling us were of course profiting from her treatment. At first they were paid by Medicaid and then by my father. The last nursing home my mother stayed in was filled four to a room with dependent elderly. Most were on feeding tubes, suffering from dementia or Alzheimer's.

My father outlived my mother by two years. Just after his 87th birthday, he finally seemed to be emerging from depression when he began to fall. First he bruised his arm. Next he broke a couple of ribs. The third time he cracked vertebrae. In the hospital he contracted pneumonia. He was transferred to a rehab and that's when he stopped eating and my sister Susan had him delivered to her apartment.

She set him up in the living room. For about a week, with help from my sister Dottie, she fed him and cared for him and he seemed to be recovering. He started eating again, sitting up and talking, and, with their help, he was able to get up out of bed and sit in a chair. He was visited by his grandchildren and his great grandchildren. Then he seemed to decide he was ready to go; he stopped eating altogether and began to fade away.

So I was there, that Sunday, two weeks after he arrived at my sister's apartment, as a visitor. By then, my sister had called a hospice nurse for help. He was on morphine and seemed to be asleep although Susan said he could hear us. Hearing, she said, is the last sense to go. When it was time to change him, she asked me to step out of the room. This was apparently to protect me from seeing my dad naked. When I returned, I held his hand a said a few words to him. That night, a few hours after I had left, my father died.

So, this is partly a cautionary tale regarding doctors, hospitals and nursing homes but it is also a tribute to my sisters for doing what each of us would like done when we're ready to go. And it's a tribute to all those daughters and hospice workers and nurses who care for our mothers and fathers, who feed them and change them and hold their hands until the end.

MARGARITA MEYENDORFF

Better known as Mourka to her friends, **Margarita Meyendorff** is the author of the published memoir *DP: Displaced Person.* The daughter of a Russian Baron, she was born displaced, far from the opulence of Imperial Russia that was her birthright. A series of wars destroyed this privileged existence, and Margarita's life became a series of extraordinary moves. She has performed as an actress, dancer, musician, and storyteller at venues throughout the United States and in Europe. Mourka is currently at work on *Flipping the Bird,* an anthology of short stories based on her numerous life adventures.

SOUP

Margarita Meyendorff

I grew up on soup. In our tiny apartment in Nyack New York, which resembled an antique store stuffed with oversized furniture, Russian *chachkas* and photographs of dead Russian aristocrats, every day we had homemade soup for lunch. In a kitchen that smelled of oil paint and turpentine because the room doubled as Papa's painting studio and bedroom, Mama would prepare the soup: potato, cabbage or borscht. After all, we were Russian refugees from a displaced persons camp, transplanted to America.

Preparing food was stressful for my mother who would prefer to write poetry or make *chachkas* from the myriad shreds of wrapping paper, fabric and furs and ribbons and threads that she kept in boxes under the beds. Mama was fighting depression and self-medicating herself with vodka and amphetamines. She was marooned in her middle years; trapped in a world not of her choosing. Mama, shell shocked and uprooted from two World Wars, found life difficult in

America with a new language, having to work in sweat shops and with the realization that her once charming Baron husband was now poor, ill and aging.

Still, the grand soup finale was unexpected. The day came when the tensions simmered and burned and with one quick gesture, she hurled my bowl of soup at me; it flew through the air like a discus and hit its target. It was hot potato soup that she threw at me the day I told her that I was leaving. The guilt I felt for not wanting to stay home to take care of my parents forced me away from the apartment, into the street. I was leaving for New York City, escaping the sickness and the sadness which permeated our tiny living space to become an actress.

I left with hot potato soup on my shoes.

Several years went by as I struggled to make a living in the theatre. Like my mother, I never liked cooking, especially for myself. I inherited some of my mother's fears, anxieties and depression. I too married a Prince Charming who would take care of me and make the fears disappear—but my Prince was also lacking—he started and lost businesses, took on strange moods and finally left me with two small children.

In the 1980's I began teaching public school. I would grab a couple of sandwiches for lunch, drop my children at their respective schools and continue on to work. It wasn't long before I became exhausted and very sick—flu, fever, and a cough that would not quit. I went to see an acupuncturist who told me that my body was cold and tired. She asked me if I had changed my diet when I started my full-time teaching job. I told her about the daily hot soups that my mother used to make when I was growing up. The acupuncturist suggested that I bring hot soup to work and eat it for lunch every day.

For the next twenty years, I brought hot soup to work on a daily basis and I never got sick. I prepared the soup from my mother's old recipes. She was long gone—I believe she expired from a hunger and a longing for a world that no longer existed.

Now, how I would love to share a bowl of soup with my Mama and thank her for the life her soups gave me. If only I could tell her how many salty tears dropped into the soup as I thought of how much Mama gave when there was little to give. If only I could tell her how peaceful I feel when I make soup. If only I could tell her, that troubled as she was, she nourished me. She gave me enough so that now, I have something to give. If only I could tell her that I love her.

ANTHONY C. MURPHY

From Lancashire, England, **Anthony C. Murphy** has worked in and on the spoken word scene in the UK and in New York City, both as a performer and an assistant producer. He was nominated for a Pushcart Prize for work in the *Westchester Review*. He has written and illustrated the children's book *Liberty Takes A Break*, and a novel, *Shiftless*. He lives in Yonkers, New York.

LUCY AND OLD FRED

Anthony C. Murphy

When I was seven years old, we moved into our first house. My baby brother had stretched the limits of space and comfort, so the council gave us a three-bedroom place on the outskirts of town. It was a red brick terrace with two stories and a mud mountain for a front lawn. This time we had lots of horizontal neighbors. It's not that they were prone to lying about on the street, we had just gotten used to the vertical kind, the upstairs crowd.

Now here, we had to make new friends, but having a dad as gregarious as ours it was easy enough. He soon knew everyone, and they knew him, and my mum, from weekends in the local pub. Those nights of old songs and singing with abandon. We could not join in then, so instead we listened after hours, waking up when they came back home clumsy and loud. We could hear the gossipy pub stories, if we were bothered to. Sometimes we heard the fights and the screaming about stuff that wasn't our fault—for once.

Old Fred lived opposite us in Number thirty-four. He was slow in his movements, and always had a cig hanging out of his mouth. He had a staggering, slobbery bulldog named Lucy who looked just like him. She didn't smoke, but it seemed like she could do, if only Old Fred could have rolled her one, or been able to bend down and light it for her. The pair of them shuffled off to the pub every evening, both gasping for air, or beer, or pork scratchings. They soon became firm family friends of ours.

As a part of the new parish, me and my older brother, J, had become Boy Scouts. Sometimes we did our bit of community service. We would clean a car for two pounds, or walk dogs for a quid, the proceeds going to the troop. We decided to ask Old Fred if he needed anything doing, any small favor or errand or chore. He said sure. We could clean his house.

His house had the smell of days. Shed dog hair and avalanched human dander, glaciers of it, covered his otherwise threadbare rug, creating a whole new look that tied the room together without any discernable visual pattern. A rank funk blanketed everything, that smell of Old Fred. The dust of a lifetime collected on forgotten or unknown knickknacks. Memory had been buried under nicotine, ash and neglect. We didn't wonder what had happened to Fred for him to live like this. He was just Old Fred. We had no clue that he had had a past life. We were just here to vacuum and polish so that we could earn another scout badge. So we went about our business, doing a great job, using our mum's cleaning products, the ones my dad hadn't drank anyway. And afterwards Fred gave us 50p. Not each, just 50p. Of course, back then we had no idea about pensions, and adults were not real humans! We knew about work. I had a paper round. I think Old Fred had a laugh to himself after he gave over that solitary, seven-sided coin though. He knew what things were worth.

Then one day Fred wasn't there anymore. Years had gone by, or at least it seemed that way. Families on the street had moved out and in and my mum had finally told my dad to leave. Fred had lasted a long time, but Lucy lasted longer. I was named in the will as the one to look after her, with a little monthly stipend for me. I had another job then. And that look in Lucy's one good, but bloodshot eye, when I brought her back after the funeral, that flicked lick at me from her jowly chops, I knew they were of thanks.

JOHN PIELMEIER

John Leonard Pielmeier began his career with the play and movie *Agnes of God*, followed by three more plays on Broadway and over twenty-five television movies and miniseries produced. Most recently he's adapted William Peter Blatty's *The Exorcist* for the stage, as well as his own novel, *Hook's Tale*, premiering in Houston in spring 2021. He has received the Humanitas, Edgar, Camie, and Christopher Awards, five Writers' Guild Award nominations, and his projects have been nominated for the Emmy and Golden Globe. His website is JohnPielmeier.com.

TWO WORDS

John Pielmeier

Six hundred fifty words aren't enough.

Sometimes a monument is enough. A thoughtful gift. A home-cooked meal. A kiss. A long embrace.

Often they cannot equal the deed; the payback is too enormous, the kindness of the giver unfathomable. Repaying a debt is expected in our society; it's fair, it's reasonable. But "the heart has its reasons," Pascal once said, "of which Reason knows nothing."

Can kindness ever be repaid?

In February of 1862 Colonel Richard Owen, a Scottish-born geologist serving in the Union Army, was put in charge of an Indiana prisoner-of-war camp for Confederate soldiers. Starvation, disease, and other atrocities abounded in these camps North *and* South; the death-rate was astronomical. Owen changed that in his camp. He brought in books for the captured and saw that they were well-fed mentally *and* physically. He helped the prisoners open a bakery. He allowed them to form sports teams, theatrical companies, glee clubs. He put them in charge of their own discipline. Virtually no one tried to escape. And when he was transferred out of this camp, the prisoners themselves petitioned the Governor, asking that Owen remain.

I know this because I was once asked to write a paean to Owen. I envisioned a glee club of prisoners singing their a cappella thanks. "A champion of liberty and justice," they sing, "He never asked for kindnesses repaid."

But they *did* repay, as best they knew how. They collected funds and after his death commissioned a monument to honor his "courtesy and kindness." A monument could never serve as sufficient pay-back, of course, but perhaps the act of *raising* it was sufficient enough: a public declaration that goodness must be acknowledged, remembered, honored.

Can kindness be repaid?

My wife saved my life once—quite literally. Is this a debt I owe her? When we were younger and at the beginning of our friendship, I paid her dental bills. By the laws of our economy, I should expect repayment over time. Is that why she married me? Is her rescuing me from the clutches of death the final payback, allowing her at last to walk away? Obviously not—she's still here. Maybe she considers my life worth *more* than her dental bills—which is debatable; nevertheless, she's hanging around until I make up the difference.

What's absurd about this metaphor is that it reduces gratitude to capitalism. It's how we're taught to think in this biblical democracy of ours. There's a logic to it: a mathematical addition and subtraction of courtesies that evens things out. Biblically, it's an eye for an eye in the *best* sense; a benevolent revenge.

But gratitude is *not* payback. Nor is it obligation. It is, in its own way, a gift.

I recently lost a friend and close business partner—not to death, but to deceit. All the time that we were friends, I now know, he was shamefully deceptive. I've lost sleep over this; I have felt and still feel myself a fool, inexplicably at fault. I'm angry, I'm sad, but what's hardest, I think, is that he did me many kindnesses over the years. And for those I am grateful. But his kindnesses and my gratitude do not excuse his crime. I am wounded, and even though he asked to see me, to explain and apologize, the bandage for this wound can't be woven by his explanation and apology. No, the weavers of my healing are you—my wife, my listeners (some strangers, some friends)—who do me the kindness of hearing and not judging. I don't need your empathy. I simply need your ears. There's no logic here. The heart has its reasons of which Reason knows nothing.

Gratitude is impossible to talk about. It can only be expressed and received. Six hundred fifty words won't do it. Two words may be enough.

Thank you.

ANDI ROSENTHAL

Andi Rosenthal is the author of the novel *The Bookseller's Sonnets*, published by Roundfire Books in 2011, which was a Hadassah Brandeis Institute book club selection and a National Jewish Book Council "Book of Note." Andi has published personal essays in Kveller, ScaryMommy, and *Reform Judaism* magazine. From 2003 to 2008, Andi was the writer of a first-person column featured on InterfaithFamily.com, and the *Westchester Jewish Chronicle*. She most recently published a selection of poetry in Volume 9 of the *Westchester Review*. In her professional life, Andi serves as a Community Mobilizer for UJA-Federation of New York and is also an accomplished musician. A lifelong resident of Westchester County, she lives in New Rochelle, New York.

THE FIRST DAY BACK

Andi Rosenthal

The bagel was still on my desk when our staff returned to work two Mondays later. Still in its waxed paper wrapper, the buttered pumpernickel was exactly where I had left it when I had picked up my work bag and quickly made my way down the hall to the elevators. An announcement over the PA system directed us to stay in our offices. But I wasn't listening. Through my office windows, I had already seen enough falling bodies to know that if I had any chance of getting home, this was it.

When I returned to my office on that bright new September morning, I was unsure of what exactly I had expected to find. My desk, as usual, was neat, orderly. My computer was off, blank, seemingly shocked into silence. I touched the worn wood of my desk, running my fingers along its smooth surface, and watched as my fingertips traced three short lines in the dust. That was when I noticed the fine layer of black soot that adorned the furniture, my chair, even the bagel.

It took me a moment to realize where the dust had come from. And another minute to remember that these ashes were not only the end of the Towers as we knew them; they were a sacred composite, made up of concrete, mercury, flesh, memory.

Having worked downtown at the Museum of Jewish Heritage—A Living Memorial to the Holocaust—for nearly two years, I and my colleagues had developed some particular and peculiar sensitivities about everyday objects and actions. For instance, when New York City had celebrated the "Cow Parade" the previous year, creating an installation of artist-designed cow statues in close proximity to city landmarks, we had to pass, thanks to the unwanted association with cattle cars. Having to live inside the perspective of genocide was part of our daily working lives, but in no way had it prepared us for what we all saw that morning.

We had watched the world change before our very eyes; eyes that were accustomed to bearing witness on a daily basis to the inhuman events that had come to shape history in the twentieth century. We never believed that in the dawn of the twenty-first, we would be present as evil prevailed again, in real time, just four blocks north.

Now, on September 24th, we were set to return to work. I pushed the button that brought my computer back to life, listening for voices, the normal patter of a workday coming to life. I placed my jacket over my chair and grabbed a few paper towels from inside my desk drawer, gingerly wiped down the desk and my keyboard, threw the bagel in the wastebasket. I thought about how normal everything had seemed that morning. And now I couldn't remember what I did, what came next, what was supposed to happen now.

The machine creaked and hummed as it loaded the data, meetings and memos that seemed to belong to another world. The calendar page opened up to the last date that it had been checked: Tuesday, September 11. I scrolled to the first email and read the message from my colleague at the Lower Manhattan Marketing Association: CANCELED: the subject line read. The email then went on: Reminder: *Our Tuesday 8:30am meeting at Top of the World (WTC2) is canceled due to Primary Day. Don't forget to vote.*

It would be another month before our beloved Museum would be open to visitors to teach about loss and heartache, and it would be a year before we found the courage and compassion to mount an exhibition in memory of those who died that September morning. But on that first day, as I heard the voices of my colleagues returning to engage in the sacred work of memory, I finally remembered why I was there: to bear witness, because I was alive.

LEANNE SOWUL

Leanne Sowul is an award-winning writer and music teacher whose writing has appeared in Hippocampus, *Confrontation, Hudson Valley* magazine, and other online and print journals. An elementary band director and highly sought-after private flute teacher, Leanne can play every woodwind, brass and percussion instrument (just don't give her a cello). In 2017, Leanne won both the Scott Meyer Award for personal essay and the All-American Dream Champion Award for music teaching. In the spirit of gratitude, Leanne expresses her deepest thanks to her former teachers, current colleagues, and all of her students in the Arlington Music Program with whom it is her lifelong honor to make music. Leanne lives with her husband and two children in the Hudson Valley, and her website is LeanneSowul.com.

THE BAND ROOM

Leanne Sowul

The low rumble of timpani mallets contrasts with the peaked pitch of teenaged voices as I enter the band room on the first day of high school. Shiny instruments emerge from cases big and small. Four half-circles of chairs and music stands face a podium, and there's a folder with my name on it in the front row. I unpack my flute on my knees and blow a few soft, experimental notes across the mouthpiece while keeping my chin low to hide the scar bisecting my neck.

The scar is fresh. Six weeks ago, a surgeon slit my throat and scooped out my thyroid gland to remove the malignant tumor wrapped around it. As my life split itself into before and after, I groped for a shred of normalcy and found it in high school marching band. I'd already signed up and gone through rookie training earlier in the summer. But band camp— required for learning routines to that year's show— was scheduled during my first week of cancer treatment. Instead of marching the field in patterns coordinated to the music I'd already memorized, tramping through mud and heat with my bandmates and giggling in bunk beds at night, I ingested radioactive iodine and spent four days isolated in a hospital room.

Today is the first time I've opened my flute case in weeks. Though the marching band director said I could play the show's music from the sidelines this season— a compromise for missing band camp—I'd said no. If I'd been given special circumstances, the whole marching band would find out why and I'd become the "cancer kid." Pity equals attention; I don't want either. If I try hard enough, maybe I can pretend the cancer doesn't exist here. Two separate worlds: one for cancer, one for school.

The Wind Ensemble director raps his baton on the conductor's stand. As talk dies down, he meets my wide-eyed gaze and awards me what I'll learn is a rare but genuine smile. He directs us to take a piece of music from our folders, then raises his baton. We breathe as one and release our first sound.

Layers of tones vibrate from woodwinds, brass and percussion. We listen for balance and intonation, then adjust. The tones condense, purify. We listen and adjust again, all without words. The next chord comes, and the next, and soon my heartbeat aligns with the beat of the baton and my skin thrums in harmony with each pitch. My summer without music left me parched, and now I'm guzzling it down. A swell of trapped emotion fights its way out of my chest and into the air of my flute.

Slowly, cautiously, I straighten my spine. I lift my chin.

The cancer will stay with me throughout high school, but only here in the band room do I allow myself to open the doors between my two worlds. I share my deepest fears with my bandmates, not with words, but with breath and tongue and silvery tone. The flutes wail their grief with me in plaintive melody. Saxophones and clarinets sing consolation; trumpets and trombones blare brassy-bright hope. The snare drum raps a strengthening cadence. Through music, we forge my soul's resting place.

The following year on the marching band field, the cancer marches with me; I'm no longer on the sidelines.

Years later, I rap my own baton on a conductor's stand and give my students a not-so-rare smile. We breathe as one and release our first sound. They pass the music between them, listening and blending, communicating their hearts through breath and tongue and silvery tone. Fears are shared, grievances aired, anxieties voiced. The band absorbs, diffuses, and transforms it all into melodious salve and harmonious joy.

I look out over the band room, watching my students. Slowly, cautiously, they straighten their spines. They lift their chins.

YVONNE STAFFORD

Yvonne Stafford has broad intellectual and creative interests and is accomplished in business, real estate development, writing, art, event planning, and community leadership. Her articles have appeared in *Crain's New York Business*, the *New York Beacon*, *New York Amsterdam News*, and *Real Estate Weekly*. She is a holistic health advocate, motivational speaker, and laughter ambassador. Noted author Gary Null, Ph.D. called her non-fiction book, *From Fast Foods to Slow Foods; How to Wake up Laughing*, "an excellent first step on your journey to health and happiness." Ms. Stafford graduated from New York University with a master's degree in communications and interdisciplinary arts and is proud to be the 2018 first-place winner of the *African Voices* magazine Flash Fiction contest.

MY FIRST JOB

Yvonne Stafford

My parents emigrated from the Caribbean to Harlem with big dreams. In our house, education was of utmost importance. It was a foregone conclusion that I would go to college. I wanted to be a dancer. However, my high school counselor said I only had two choices. Dancer was not one of them. She said I could be a nurse or a teacher. I chose teacher.

I went to college in upstate New York, joined the dance club, passed all my academic classes with honors, and graduated as a teacher. When I came back home, I enrolled in an African Dance School.

One day my friend's mother, who was the principal of an elementary school on Vyse Avenue in the South Bronx, called me.

"What are you doing now Yvonne? Do you have a job"? "Yes, I am studying African Dance." "I need you to teach a class at my school. We have an overage of students in the sixth grade." My parents were thrilled. Each teacher was

allowed to send four children to the new class, 6E—my assign-
ment—a class of discarded students. I got all the good kids.
My only experience in a classroom was student teaching in
Albany, New York.

First Day: The teacher in the next room kept her class
in order by screaming at them. "Stand straight and stop
talking. Didn't I tell you to stay in line?" Scared me half to
death.

Right off the bat, every time I began to speak, Juan
Ruiz, sitting in the front row, started making mocking noises
and drumming on his desk.

"Whoop woo," He wouldn't stop. "Beep-taaah" I ran
over and grabbed his shoulders. My fingernail accidently
scratched his neck.

"I'm going to tell my mother!" He yelled.

"I'm sorry about the accident, Juan"

Not a problem. I knew about parent/teacher meetings
from my Albany experience. The next day, Juan came to school
in a turtleneck sweater. He looked up at me.

"I didn't tell my Mother."

Juan became my security, protector and friend. If anyone looked like they might get out of line, all Juan had to do
was give them the look that could kill.

What did we do all year? I brought forth lessons from
home. We told stories. We became the stories. We broke down
big words, like *actions, consequences, responsibility, compassion,
blame, shame, bully, disappointment, faith, struggle, and gratitude,*
by doing small improvisations. We talked about my parents'

dreams and of people who looked like us whose dreams, actions and inventions made the world better. We saw maps and pictures of the world beyond the South Bronx.

They taught me about home and living in the South Bronx. I found out the reason Roberto had a black eye was because he got in the way of a blow meant for his mother. I found out the reason Florence talked so loudly was because she lived in an apartment building where the elevated subway passed all hours of the day and night. I found out that Thomas needed to know he had to wash his own shirt so he would not be bullied for smelling.

What did I learn? I learned to truly listen. I learned listening without judgment and showing love was more important than yelling to keep order.

Last Day: They told me that I did not act like a teacher. "Well, what do I act like?"

"You act like a Mommy."

Twenty-Five Years Later: A young woman came up to me.

"I know you," she said. "Really, from where?" "You were my sixth-grade teacher."

"I am a dancer."

"Vyse Avenue, South Bronx. I remember 6E. You were my sixth-grade teacher."

I am grateful for what I learned as a teacher for one year in the South Bronx. I am grateful for the Mommy designation and the good-bye hugs. I am grateful to be alive.

XAVIER TREVINO

Xavier Trevino has been in recovery for nineteen years and, after a lifetime of menial jobs, he's started to rekindle his dream of being a writer. He has taken writing courses at JCC Manhattan and lives with his wife, Danusia, in Washington Heights, New York City.

TURKEY

Xavier Trevino

I'd been handed sheets with Christmas carols when I walked in the basement of a storefront church on West 47th Street. One of those sad little places where you look in the window and see people shaking tambourines. Christ, I thought. I was going to have to listen to this as well as a sermon.

I sat down on a hard, wooden pew with a bunch of other forlorn rejects, men mostly but a few women, alcoholics, drug addicts, and the mentally ill. We were all waiting for the free turkey my father told me we were entitled to.

On the stage, an enormous bald man sat behind the organ. His thin, flaccid arms jutted from his short sleeves.

Then an energetic, fit man in his forties stepped up to the lectern. "Welcome! I'm Pastor Juan, and I want to remind you that you are all God's children and Jesus loves you."

He spoke about God, love, sin, and redemption. I wanted to laugh. I'd stopped believing in Jesus a long time ago.

I was a recovering heroin addict, on a methadone program, just divorced, with no place to live except my aging alcoholic father's squalid apartment. This felt ridiculous, waiting for a turkey he had to have, doing it not just because I was living in his home, but because I was so lonely, I was willing to sit in a basement filled with society's rejects. And I was one of them!

How did I get here? I knew the answer. Everything I touched turned to crap. I knew I was just a step above the guy sitting next to me with no teeth who smelled like stale gin. I, a forty-six-year-old living with his father.

The pastor walked off the stage. The enormous man began to play and sing. I listened to his falsetto voice. The audience chimed in. Raggedly.

Not me. I leafed through the sheets, fifteen or so songs. It was clear this turkey was going to cost me most of the afternoon.

We got to the "Gloria" song. I had always liked it; the way "Gloria" was stretched out. At the second refrain, I got up my nerve to join in.

"Gloria ..." I sang, flat and off-key.

By the third verse, my voice started to crack, and I could feel tears welling. I tried to stop crying but it was no use. I was totally broken inside and the tears ran.

Suddenly I felt loved. I didn't know by whom. Couldn't be Jesus, because I didn't believe in him. Maybe by the gin-smelling guy who actually smiled at me when I started to sing, or the fat man behind the organ who at some point looked at me and nodded, or maybe Pastor Juan, lurking somewhere in the back.

After "Joy to the World," the organist turned off his instrument and we headed upstairs.

As we shuffled along, I was glad my moment of sadness was over. The smell of the basement and people were starting to get to me.

Upstairs were big cardboard boxes filled with turkeys.

"Jesus loves you, brother!" Pastor Juan said as he handed me a boxed turkey.

"Sure," I mumbled and turned away.

Walking up 47th Street, I started crying again. People passed by me, their faces blurred as I made my way through my story of loss, shame and disappointment. I was a divorced college educated man mopping floors for a living.

That evening, I went to my self-help group. The guy who ran things laid out plans for a group Thanksgiving dinner. "If anyone can bring a dish, that would be great," he said.

"I can bring a turkey," I said impulsively, grateful to have something to contribute. All heads turned my way. I finally felt like I belonged somewhere.

FRANCES TUNNO

Frances Tunno currently works as a copywriter, but she is also a freelance writer, voice actress, blogger and mother of three. She's been voicing radio and TV commercials for decades and was a morning news and traffic reporter in Los Angeles for twelve years. She was one of the BlogHer 2015 Voices of the Year for her post, "I Was 21 Before My Father Told me He Loved Me," which can be found on her blog, AtFransTable.com. Fran writes about life, family, her Italian family, and food; she currently lives in Los Angeles, California.

I'M NOT ELLEN DeGENERES

Frances Tunno

I always thought that one day I'd do something that would make me exceptional. But I'm 59 years old and am not exceptional yet, so things aren't looking terribly promising. I don't live in my lovely home anymore; job loss and a divorce took care of that.

I feel like I never really achieved serious success in any of my jobs. I was a sales rep and was okay. I was a news and traffic reporter and was pretty good. I'm still a copywriter and am pretty good. I'm a voice actress and audiobook narrator and I'm pretty good. I'm a blogger and thought that might be where I'd really shine, but exceptional? Not yet.

So, I'm pretty good at a lot of things, exceptional at nothing so far. I'm not saying this for sympathy; it's just how I feel, which is really hard to admit.

And I keep asking for a sign. I keep hoping something will happen that says, "HEY, YOU'RE ON THE RIGHT TRACK. Stick with this performance and writing thing, something good is coming!"

But I get no sign, no burning bush—nothing. And publishers don't come looking for you; you have to find them. Writing takes skill, diligence and unbelievably constant self-promotion.

I would never admit this self-doubt to my twenty-something kids. Why add to their stress? It's bad enough they feel insecure sometimes. I'm *their* cheerleader, I can't fall apart. Besides, they've already witnessed my wilting self-esteem more times than I care to admit.

So, tonight, when my daughter and I got home, and we found my son here, it just seemed like a normal night. He was grouchy because he hadn't eaten anything all day and feeling bad that he hadn't been able to put the final touches on my computer, which he promised to have fixed yesterday. And my daughter was tired and starving, as usual.

So, I strode into the kitchen in full mother-mode because like my Italian mom before me, I know most everything can be cured with food. I patched up a salad from last night's leftovers. I put yesterday's grocery store roasted chicken on top of some quinoa salad and added homemade salad dressing. My son devoured that and my daughter's lumpy, leftover burrito. I made some espresso for a quick latte for my daughter, who subsists primarily on caffeine. Then she popped popcorn while my son was diving into my banana bread with chocolate chips.

Not a gourmet dinner, but they were happy. My son told me my banana bread with chocolate chips was godly.

They sat in the sunlight talking and eating while I watched.

They looked so beautiful I took a photo. Then my son got up, walked over and wrapped me in a big hug. He apologized for being grouchy and not finishing my computer. He told me the food was great and that I was a good mom.

As I stood hugging him, with the afternoon sunlight shining on us in this small 1930s kitchen, I thought: *Wow, this feels so nice. Maybe this is the sign! My kids are good kids. They're kind, loving and good. Maybe I am a success at this, maybe* **this** *is what I'm here to do. Maybe my mothering will have a more lasting effect than anything else I'm pursuing.*

I've never felt more grateful.

Maybe I don't have to be exceptional on the world's stage. Maybe I don't need a big house. Maybe I can relax a little knowing that being a good mom to my kids, who seem to be turning out okay, *is* my job. Maybe I don't have to be the next Ellen DeGeneres or Nora Ephron to be considered a success. Maybe just being the good mom that my mom taught me to be is what I'm here to do. And maybe I'm starting to be okay with that.

SARAH BRACEY WHITE

Sarah Bracey White is a writer, teacher, and arts consultant. She earned degrees from Morgan State University and the University of Maryland. She was an Inaugural Fellow at the Purchase College Writers Center. Her published works include *Primary Lessons: A Memoir, The Wanderlust: A South Carolina Folk Tale,* and *Feelings Brought to Surface,* a poetry collection. Her essays have been anthologized in *Children of the Dream, Dreaming in Color, Living in Black and White, Aunties: 35 Writers Celebrate Their Other Mother, Gardening on a Deeper Level,* and *Heartscapes: True Stories of Remembered Loves.* The *New York Times,* the *Afro-American Newspapers* and the *Journal News* have published her essays. Sarah is a frequent contributor to Read650. She and her husband live in Ossining, New York.

FOR THINGS DENIED

Sarah Bracey White

Most people are grateful for the things they've been
given. While I too have been given innumerable concrete
and intangible things for which I'm thankful, those aren't the
blessings I celebrate most. I'm most grateful for the denial of
things I desired. Looking back, I remember times I zealously
prayed for my return to the childhood home I shared with
my aunt and uncle in Philadelphia. As a head-strong and
heart-challenged child, I didn't possess the insight to compre-
hend the meaning of my mother's words, *Be careful what you
wish for, you just might get it*. I didn't know that while the great
Northern Migration offered the opportunity for advancement,
it robbed many people of a sense of home, community, and an
attachment to the land of their birth.

My mother's refusal to abandon those things guar-
anteed that I would benefit from them, despite the pain that
education carried. Separated from my cossetted Philadelphia
world, I was thrust into life's turbulent waters at an early age

where I floundered until I learned to swim. *A child rises to the level of a teacher's expectations*, my mother often said. Her school-teacher friends made sure that I received a superior early education. But I wasn't just *educated* in my segregated classrooms. I was challenged to be everything I could be and made aware of the racist system that required me to do better and be better than white children—to get half of what they got.

I regularly prayed for my absentee father's return. I didn't know that my older sisters had prayed that same prayer—and had it granted. Our father had twice before reappeared, then quickly disappeared from our home, leaving yet another baby growing in our mother's belly. Mine was a child's desire for a father who would ease our family's burdens, not add to them.

As a teen, I longed for the freedom to go to house parties, football games, and the ice cream shop where my friends hung out on Saturday afternoons. But those things were forbidden to me. My carefully supervised world revolved around school, household chores, church and books. I graduated near the top of my class. Many of my girlfriends who had more lenient mothers found themselves pregnant before high-school graduation or embarking on early, short-lived marriages.

Ever yearning for a father, I begged my careworn, but still beautiful mother to divorce my father and find another husband—one who would take care of us. She never did. As a result, I never had to fight off the unwanted advances of her potential suitors, the way several girlfriends, in later years, told me they did.

I thought the constraints and responsibilities of marriage weren't for me. So, after college, I took the civil service exam for a job at the Social Security Administration. I must have failed the test, because I never got a call-back for an interview. I'm grateful for that. A boring desk job may have offered security, benefits and a pension, but I now know it would have crushed my creative spirit.

I'm also grateful that I didn't get my teen-age wish for a husbandless life. I thought that staying single would allow me the freedom to be who I wanted to be, not who society dictated I should be. I didn't know I'd be lonely. In my mid-40s, a man whose skin color didn't match mine wooed me to the altar. He is my ever-faithful gift, the husband I never knew I wanted. For twenty-nine years, he has guarded my spirit and pushed me to soar beyond the confines of my own narrow vision.

In youth, we can neither see the valuable components of the circumstances in which we find ourselves, nor know the power those circumstances hold. I am eternally grateful that God in all his wisdom knew better than I did what it took to make me whole.

EDWARD McCANN
Read650 Founder

ACKNOWLEDGMENTS

In addition to the contributors to this volume—and all the writers who submitted their work—I thank Adriaan Fuchs, Carnegie Hall's Director of Festivals and Special Projects, for including Read650 in its Beethoven Celebration, acknowledging the 250th anniversary of the composer's birth. **CarnegieHall.org**

I'm grateful for the generosity and collaborative spirit of Evan Leslie, Artistic Producer for The New York Public Library for the Performing Arts at Lincoln Center, who partnered with Read650 to develop his vision for a special public program combining classical music with the spoken word. **NYPL.org**

My thanks to conductor and fellow collaborator Dongmin Kim, founder and Music Director of the New York Classical Players, a nonprofit organization devoted to bringing free, high-level classical music concerts to communities throughout the greater New York City metropolitan area. **NYCPmusic.org / DongminKim.com**

I so appreciate the talents of Read650 editors Karen Dukess, Steven Lewis, David Masello, and Lisa Donati Mayer for their help in curating this volume, and for the gift of copyeditor Shelley Sadler Kenny's valuable time and trained eye. Thank you all for making Read650 sound—and look—so good. **SSKenney@optonline.net**

Finally, my very special thanks to nonprofits consultant and strategist Susan Ragusa, whose free monthly Nonprofits TALK strengthens the Hudson Valley's nonprofit community through workshop and trainings addressing common organizational challenges. **SusanJRagusa.com**

READ650.ORG

INFO@READ650.ORG
FACEBOOK.COM/READ650

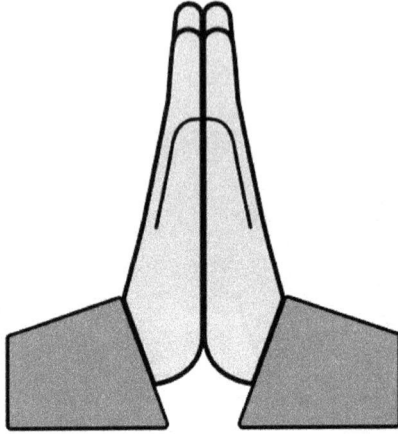

www.ingramcontent.com/pod-product-compliance
Lightning Source LLC
Chambersburg PA
CBHW060328050426
42449CB00011B/2700